SAMUEL FREN

OTHER PEOPLE'S MONEY

A PLAY IN TWO ACTS
BY JERRY STERNER

OTHER PEOPLE'S MONEY

A PLAY IN TWO ACTS

By
JERRY STERNER

SAMUEL FRENCH, INC.
45 West 25th Street   NEW YORK 10010
7623 Sunset Boulevard HOLLYWOOD 90046
LONDON   TORONTO

IMPORTANT BILLING AND CREDIT REQUIREMENTS

All producers of OTHER PEOPLE'S MONEY *must* give credit to the Author of the Play in all programs distributed in connection with performances of the Play and in all instances in which the title of the Play appears for purposes of advertising, publicizing or otherwise exploiting the Play and/or a production. The name of the Author *must* also appear on a separate line, in which no other name appears, immediately following the title, and *must* appear in size of type not less than fifty percent the size of the title type.

IN ADDITION, the following credits *must* appear in all programs, in substantially the following form:

OTHER PEOPLE'S MONEY was originally presented by the American Stage Company, Teaneck, New Jersey.

The play was subsequently presented by Hartford Stage Company.

Note: The name Hartford Stage Company *must* appear on a line immediately below the name American Stage Company and *must* be in size of type the same as American Stage Company.

MUSIC ROYALTY

In addition to the play royalty, there is a music royalty charge of $3.50 per performance for amateur groups (stock music royalty quoted upon application) for the use of the song "The Farmer and the Cowman" in productions of OTHER PEOPLE'S MONEY.

American Stage

C O M P A N Y

in residence at Fairleigh Dickinson University

Paul Sorvino, Artistic Director
Theodore Rawlins, Producing Director
James R. Singer, Producing Director

presents

The World Premiere Of

OTHER PEOPLE'S MONEY

by

Jerry Sterner

featuring

Katherine Cortez	Henderson Forsythe	Keith Langsdale
Stanja Lowe	**David Schramm**	**Ben Sweetwood**

Directed by

John Ferraro

Set Designer	Lighting Designer	Costume Designer
Daniel Ettinger	**Stuart Duke**	**Joan V. Evans**

Production Stage Manager	Casting by
Nereida Ortiz	**Judy Henderson & Associates**

May 2 - May 24, 1987
Produced by Special Arrangement with Jeffrey Ash

THE CAST
(in order of appearance)

WILLIAM COLES . . . . Keith Langsdale*

ANDREW JORGENSON . . . . Henderson Forsythe*

BEA SULLIVAN . . . . Stanja Lowe*

LAWRENCE GARFINKLE . . . . David Schramm*

KATE SULLIVAN . . . . Katherine Cortez*

ARTHUR . . . . Ben Sweetwood

*Performers and stage managers are members of Actors' Equity Association, the Union of Professional Actors and Stage Managers in the United States.

The Time: The present
The Place: New York and Rhode Island

There will be one fifteen minute intermission.

This production is the world premiere of *Other People's Money*.

Hartford Stage

Mark Lamos, Artistic Director
David Hawkanson, Managing Director

Other People's Money
by Jerry Sterner
Director—Gloria Muzio
Set Designer—David Jenkins
Costume Designer—Jess Goldstein
Lighting Designer—F. Mitchell Dana
Sound Designer—David Budries
Production Stage Manager—Stacey Fleischer

CAST
William Coles—James Murtaugh
Andrew Jorgenson—Arch Johnson
Bea Sullivan—Scotty Bloch
Lawrence Garfinkle—Jon Polito
Kate Sullivan—Mercedes Ruehl

Casting—David Tochterman Casting
David Tochterman/Julie Mossberg
In association with
Judy Henderson Casting

Presented by special arrangement with
Jeffrey Ash and Susan Quint Gallin

*"Other People's Money" takes place in New York
and Rhode Island.*

There will be one intermission.

*"Other People's Money" was originally presented
by the American Stage Company, Teaneck, NJ.*

*This production is underwritten in part
by a grant from the
GREATER HARTFORD ARTS COUNCIL
and its 1,550 corporate contributors.*

MINETTA LANE THEATRE

An M Square Entertainment, Inc. Theatre

JEFFREY ASH and SUSAN QUINT GALLIN
in association with DENNIS GRIMALDI present
The HARTFORD STAGE COMPANY Production of

OTHER PEOPLE'S MONEY

...the ultimate seduction

A New Play by
JERRY STERNER

with

KEVIN CONWAY   SCOTTY BLOCH   ARCH JOHNSON

JAMES MURTAUGH   MERCEDES RUEHL

Scenic Designer
DAVID JENKINS

Costume Designer
JESS GOLDSTEIN

Lighting Designer
F. MITCHELL DANA

Sound Designer
DAVID BUDRIES

Production Stage Manager
STACEY FLEISCHER

Casting by
JUDY HENDERSON CASTING
Judy Henderson, CSA & Alycia Aumuller

Original Hartford Stage Casting by
DAVID TOCHTERMAN CASTING
David Tochterman / Julie Mossberg

Originally Presented by the
AMERICAN STAGE COMPANY
Associate Producers Michael Mathis and Our Money Productions.

Directed by
GLORIA MUZIO

CHARACTERS

WILLIAM COLES
Mid-forties. Attractive, polished, President of New England Wire and Cable.

ANDREW JORGENSON
Chairman of New England Wire and Cable, 68 years of age.

BEA SULLIVAN
Longtime assistant and friend of Jorgenson. An attractive woman in her early sixties.

LAWRENCE GARFINKLE
An obese, elegant, cunning New York "takeover artist." About forty. Hails from the Bronx and speaks in a "New York" accent.

KATE SULLIVAN
Bea's daughter. An attractive, sexy, Wall Street attorney, about thirty-five.

SETTING

New York and Rhode Island.

TIME

The Present.

OTHER PEOPLE'S MONEY

ACT I

*We hear two long bursts of a factory whistle followed by some 15
    seconds or so of music with a driving tempo incorporating
    sounds of an industrial plant during the working day. Music
    stops suddenly. BILL COLES is Centerstage with a
    spotlight on him. All else is dark.*

COLES. It's been said that you have to be a storyteller
to tell a story. It's also been said that businessmen aren't
good storytellers ... not that we don't have a story to tell ..
we do. We tell it in numbers: you know, sales, earnings,
dividends. We also express it in ratios: net worth to long
term debt, long term debt to working capital. And we tell
it every year. Have you ever read an Annual Report? ...
We're not good storytellers. Which is too bad. For there's
an important story that needs to be told. It goes way
beyond numbers. It's about loyalty, tradition, friendship
and of course, money. Lots of money. It's one heck of a
story. And if it hasn't already affected your life, it will. It
affected mine. It only started a few years back. We were
all naive then. But, you know something? I knew. I knew
as soon as the old man told me about our expected
visitor.

*(Lights up on ANDREW JORGENSON'S office Upstage Right.
He is seated behind his modest desk. Two steps down is the New
England Wire & Cable Conference Room, which extends all the*

11

way Stage Right. It is dominated by a large table. Unseen at this time, is GARFINKLE'S office Downstage Right. It has a desk and chair, a chair for a visitor, and a separate table with a stockquote machine. Along the perimeter of the stage, U-shaped, is the area GARFINKLE roams. JORGENSON is a "hand's on" type, more comfortable with his sleeves rolled up tinkering with a machine than sitting in a boardroom.)

JORGENSON. Why are you so nervous? Stop acting like an expectant father.

COLES. *(Entering from Center Stage)* I heard that name before.

JORGENSON. So what?

COLES. Why would he come all the way from New York? We've never had anyone from New York before.

JORGENSON. Sure we have. Had someone directly from Wall Street a couple of years back.

COLES. I've been here twelve years. I've never seen anyone south of Connecticut.

JORGENSON. ... Twelve years? Has it been that long? ... The guy was sitting right there — all stiff and proper taking notes on a clipboard. Some kind of analyst. Wouldn't get close to any of the walls. Scared of a little dust. Three piece suit, pointy shoes, tie up to here. He starts asking me all kinds of questions and I noticed he wasn't looking at me, looking at the wall back there. I turn around and wouldn't you know — meanest looking spider was halfway up the ceiling. You know what he says? Bill, you listening? He says, "Could you please get someone to dispose of it?" Not kill it, mind you — dispose of it. I told him since he was the one with the pointy shoes the job was his. *(Laughs at the memory.)* Didn't ask another question. Got up and left. Didn't even say goodbye.

COLES. Be careful what you say to him.

JORGENSON. Don't worry about me. Better check for spiders. *(Rises, puts arm around COLES'S shoulder.)* C'mon. C'mon. I was joking. I've never seen you this way.

COLES. Let me do the talking.

JORGENSON. You do the talking. I'll do the listening. "Nu Yawkas" are fun to listen to ... Where the hell was that guy from? ... Aha — Barney Smith.

COLES. Smith, Barney.

JORGENSON. Smith, Barney. Figures. Wall Street generally does things ass backwards.

COLES. Have you looked at our stock lately?

JORGENSON. I already got a call from Ozzie at the bank. Happier than a pig in shit. Told me it's up a couple of points. He owns fifteen thousand shares, you know. Has for years. I remember the day he bought. Same day I was made President. I was really scared. He called. Told me he was buying the stock to show his confidence in me. Told me he wouldn't sell till I retired. The man kept his word for ... thirty-eight years now.

COLES. More shares traded in the last month than did all last year.

JORGENSON. Bill, what's wrong with you? The stock is going up. Worry when the stock goes down.

(BEA Enters hurriedly. She's excited. BEA is an attractive woman in her early sixties.)

BEA. Come. Look. Look! *(She ushers them quickly to an imaginary window Downstage.)* Is that something, Jorgy?

JORGENSON. That's a god damned big car.

COLES. It's a stretch limo.

BEA. *(to JORGENSON:)* You see — manners. The chauffeur gets out first, walks all the way around ... opens the door. You could learn from that, Jorgy.

JORGENSON. God damned big car.

(Lights up on GARFINKLE, cross stage. He is an immense man of forty, though he looks older. He is always elegantly dressed, surprisingly graceful for his bulk. He is in some way, larger than life. His deep, rich voice fills the stage. He speaks in a New York rhythm. He looks about.)

GARFINKLE. Haven't seen a place this shitty since I left the Bronx.

BEA. *(moving to GARFINKLE, her hand extended)* Welcome. You must be Lawrence Garfinkle. I'm Bea Sullivan. Mr. Jorgenson's assistant. He's expecting you. *(She shakes his hand. They begin walking to JORGENSON'S office.)* Would you like to invite your chauffeur in? We have a small reception area where he could wait — keep warm.

GARFINKLE. He's a "yard" chauffeur. Bring him inside and you'll spoil him.

BEA. ... Right this way please. *(They Enter office.)* This is Mr. Jorgenson, our Chairman. Mr. Coles, our President. Mr. Garfinkle.

JORGENSON. Call me Jorgy. Everyone else does. *(Moves from his desk. They shake.)* Welcome to New England Wire and Cable.

COLES. How do you do, Mr. Garfinkle?

GARFINKLE. I do good. Mind if I have a seat? I do even better when I sit.

JORGENSON. *(Laughs.)* I know what you mean. *(GAR-FINKLE dusts off chair in conference room with a handkerchief.)* Uh-oh, Bill ... Better check for spiders. *(moving to GAR-FINKLE)* Wire and Cable is man's work. Gotta expect a little grime.

BEA. May I get you some coffee?

GARFINKLE. Is there a Dunkin' Donuts in this town?

BEA. Dunkin' Donuts?...

JORGENSON. Never saw one.

GARFINKLE. Crispy Cremes? ... Something?

JORGENSON. There's Sam's on Beaver. Doesn't he make donuts?

BEA. I believe he does. He'd be your best bet. Just make a left when you leave the plant. Beaver is your second—

GARFINKLE. *(taking a large roll of cash from his pocket and handing BEA several bills)* Why don't you be a sweetheart and take a ride with Arthur and pick up a couple of dozen. Bring one here and leave one in the car for the trip back.

BEA. ... They might not have much of a selection. Which kind do you like?

GARFINKLE. I like them all. *(smiling for the first time)* Can't you tell? *(BEA Exits.)*

JORGENSON. Have a nice ride, Bea. You watch, she's going to take him the long way to Beaver. What'd you say your first name was?

GARFINKLE. Lawrence.

JORGENSON. Larry, you made her day. Last limo we saw up here was in '48 when Harry Truman was running for President. Came right here to the plant. Come, I'll show you. *(Takes him to imaginary window downstage.)* Stood right out there. Right there. Gave a speech. Just after the war. It was the golden age, rebuilding America and all. Had thirty five hundred men working right here. Right at this plant. Going twenty-four hours a day, seven days a week. Truman gave a fine talk. Very impressive. Only Democrat I ever voted for.

COLES. What can we do for you, Mr. Garfinkle? What brings a busy man like you up this way?

GARFINKLE. Harry Truman stories don't grab you, huh?

COLES. We're all busy.

GARFINKLE. You're right. Let's do business. I got a computer back in New York. Call her Carmen. Every morning when I wake up — before I even brush my teeth, I punch out "Carmen computer on the wall, who's the fairest of them all?" You'll forgive me — my programmer isn't Shakespeare.

COLES. Go on.

GARFINKLE. Most mornings she spits out "You are, Garfinkle, you're the fairest of them all." But once in a while, maybe two, three times a year she says something else. Six weeks ago she said: "Garfinkle, Garfinkle, scratch your balls, New England Wire and Cable is the fairest of them all." *(JORGENSON laughs.)* I thought it was funny too. "Wire and Cable — gross me out." I yell back to Carmen. And I do it again. "Carmen computer on the wall, who's the fairest of them all?" She responds, "Don't be a schmuck, Garfinkle — do the numbers!"

COLES. I'm interested. Do the numbers.

GARFINKLE. Get a paper and pencil. Carmen will educate you. *(COLES takes a pad and pencil from JORGEN-*

SON'S desk.) The Wire and Cable business is a little soft. Has been for the last ten years. What's it worth?

JORGENSON. This would not be a good time to—

GARFINKLE. I know. I'm not blaming you. You've done a hell of a job. You've kept it alive. That's an accomplishment. Carmen agrees. I'll bet she thinks it's worth more than you do. She says you got equipment up here that cost 120 million. Worth, even at salvage 30-35 million. Write down 30 million. How many acres you got here?

COLES. One hundred ten.

GARFINKLE. What's that worth?

JORGENSON. It would depend on what it's used for.

GARFINKLE. Worst case basis. Grazing land. Ten million fair? *(COLES nods.)* Good. Write down ten. Put it underneath the thirty.

JORGENSON. We have other businesses, you know. Bill here has diversified us a good deal. He's done a hell of a job, despite my kicking and screaming.

COLES. What does Carmen think the rest of the company is worth, Mr. Garfinkle?

GARFINKLE. Let's see ... What do you got? Plumbing supplies, electrical distribution, adhesives ... boring. Nothing my friends on the street would get excited about. But dependable. Decent cash flow.

JORGENSON. With our cumulative losses at Wire and Cable we keep all the earnings from our other businesses. We haven't paid Federal taxes in years.

GARFINKLE. You haven't made money in years.

JORGENSON. It'll turn. We got a good crew up here. Best in the business. When it does we're gonna knock their socks off.

GARFINKLE. Everything is possible. Maybe a Dunkin' Donuts will open up next door.

COLES. What does your computer tell you the rest of our businesses are worth, Mr. Garfinkle.

GARFINKLE. Conservative ... six times cash flow.

COLES. We had ten million in flow last year. This year we're projecting a fifteen per cent—

GARFINKLE. Carmen only knows what happened. She can't predict. Write down sixty ... underneath the ten.

COLES. What else, Mr. Garfinkle?

GARFINKLE. Working capital. You got twenty-five million — ten million of it in cash — write down twenty-five.

COLES. Anything else?

GARFINKLE. Add it up. What do you got?

COLES. One hundred and twenty-five million.

GARFINKLE. Good. Now let's say Carmen was suffering from pre-menstrual syndrome. *(JORGENSON looks at him quizzically.)* A little crazed. Too optimistic. Forget twenty-five million. Take it off. What do you got?

COLES. One hundred million.

GARFINKLE. Nice round number. I like nice round numbers. Now make a line. Right down the middle of the page. Start a new column. Call it liabilities. Let's see what you got. Any debt?

JORGENSON. Not a penny. Don't believe in it.

GARFINKLE. Any lawsuits? Any environmental bull-shit?

JORGENSON. None. We've complied with every law. That's a good part of our losses right there.

GARFINKLE. Pension liabilities?

COLES. Fully funded.

GARFINKLE. OK. Add it up. What do you got?

JORGENSON. Didn't write anything.

GARFINKLE. That's exactly what I said to Carmen. Now here comes the fun part. How many shares you got outstanding?

COLES. Four million.

GARFINKLE. Divide four million into the hundred million. What do you got?

COLES. Twenty-five.

GARFINKLE. Good. Now that was all foreplay. Let's go for the real thing. What's your stock selling at?

COLES. You know very well what it's selling at, Mr. Garfinkle.

GARFINKLE. Aw, don't do that. I came all the way from New York. Don't break my rhythm. Let me do my thing. What's the stock at?

COLES. Ten — before you started buying.

GARFINKLE. That's a ten for a twenty-five dollar number. Forty cents on the dollar. Carmen almost came! ...I had to change my underwear.

JORGENSON. This is a fine company, Larry. We've worked hard. We have a nice story to tell but unless you make those little micro-chips or fry chicken it's hard to interest you money guys on Wall Street.

COLES. How many shares have you bought, Mr. Garfinkle?

GARFINKLE. One hundred and ninety-six thousand. I recognize a good job when I see it. I'm happy to put my money here.

JORGENSON. *(laughing)* I'll have to tell Ozzie at the

bank. He'll be mighty grateful to you. If you have time we'll have lunch together. Get him to spring for it. Tell him you're selling if he don't spring for it. Ozzie's tighter than a duck's ass. How'd you figure out to buy such an odd amount? Why not two hundred thousand — nice even number. Thought you liked nice even numbers.

COLES. Two hundred thousand is five per cent of our shares. At five per cent he has to file a 13-D with the Securities and Exchange Commission. It becomes public knowledge. *(to GARFINKLE:)* Plan on buying more?

GARFINKLE. Never can tell. Got to talk to Carmen.

JORGENSON. That's his business, Bill. He'll let us know when he wants to ... or when he has to. It's nice to know you have that confidence in us. Nice to have you as a stockholder.

GARFINKLE. Don't let me down. Get us to twenty-five. That's what we're worth.

JORGENSON. You know I can't control that. We do the best we can running the company. I can promise you one thing — we spend the stockholder's money with care. We don't squander it.

GARFINKLE. Not on paint at any rate.

JORGENSON. Not on anything. You watch the nickels and dimes and the dollars take care of themselves. My dad always said that. He founded this company. I guess I do too. As true today as when he said it.

(BEA Enters with a bag of donuts.)

JORGENSON. Bea, Larry here is our newest stockholder.

Give the man a donut.

BEA. All they had were honey and whole wheat. I left six of each in the car. *(She holds out bag. GARFINKLE takes one out, grimaces and puts it back.)*

JORGENSON. How was the ride?

BEA. Everyone stared. It's got a television, a bar, telephone, stock quote machine—

JORGENSON. And now donuts. If you have no objection, Larry, we're going to call you the "donut man."

GARFINKLE. Where's my change?

BEA. *(handing him the change)* Oh — I'm sorry. Just a little flustered, I guess ... sorry.

GARFINKLE. I like to watch the nickels and dimes too. *(GARFINKLE takes the bag and Exits the playing area. They stare after him for a beat.)*

JORGENSON. So, you really like being chauffeured around? I thought you'd be embarrassed.

BEA. Jorgy, riding in a limousine is not an acquired taste. One takes to it all at once.

(Lights out in JORGENSON'S office. Lights up Downstage Left. GARFINKLE is alone checking out the donuts.)

GARFINKLE. Whole wheat and honey. What — do I look sick? You eat this when you're sick — with tea. *(GAR-FINKLE moves toward his office.)* Step on it, Arthur. This whole god damned place stinks. Make sure you get the car washed when we get home.

(COLES moves to Center Stage. Lights up on GARFINKLE'S office as COLES Enters.)

COLES. That's an impressive office you have out there.

GARFINKLE. No big deal. Only lawyers. What can I do for you?

COLES. Thanks for seeing me on such short notice. I'm not really here on business. My wife and I came down to spend the evening with Bill, Jr. He's attending Columbia. Got two more after him. Both girls. Claire's out shopping now. It's always a treat to come to this city.

GARFINKLE. Great.

COLES. We're from small towns in Florida. Met at Florida State.

GARFINKLE. What'd you come here for — to give me your biography?

COLES. I didn't know I was boring you.

GARFINKLE. Now you know.

COLES. *(trying to control himself)* ... I'll get to the point. I see by the latest 13-D you hold just over four hundred thousand shares. That's ten per cent.

GARFINKLE. Four hundred and twenty-five thousand. Bought some this morning.

COLES. The filing says they were purchased for "investment purposes only."

GARFINKLE. I never read filings.

COLES. What does "investment purposes only" mean?

GARFINKLE. Means I bought them to make money.

COLES. How much more do you intend on buying?

GARFINKLE. That's none of your business.

COLES. Can we speak frankly?

GARFINKLE. No. Lie to me. Tell me how thrilled you

are to know me. Tell me how gorgeous I am.

COLES. You don't want to speak frankly?

GARFINKLE. I always speak frankly. I don't like people who say "Can we speak frankly?" Means they're bullshitting me the rest of the time.

COLES. I'm sorry. I won't use that phrase anymore.

GARFINKLE. What do you want?

COLES. Two years. I want two years.

GARFINKLE. For what?

COLES. Jorgenson is sixty-eight. In two years he'll be seventy. He steps down at seventy.

GARFINKLE. Says who?

COLES. It's an agreement he has with the Board. His employment contract expires at seventy.

GARFINKLE. The Board are his cronies. He is the Board. What he wants done gets done.

COLES. He gave me his word. He's a man of his word.

GARFINKLE. Stop playing with yourself.

COLES. Twelve years ago he told me if I did the job it'd be my company to run when he steps down. That's why I came to that Godforsaken place. It's the same reason I'm here. I don't want the rug pulled out from under me so close to the finish line.

GARFINKLE. You're wasting your time. I don't have two years.

COLES. Listen, Mr. Garfinkle. I said we could grow our other businesses by fifteen per cent. I was being conservative. We'll grow them in excess of twenty. I can manage. I can manage the hell out of a company. In two years we'll be worth considerably more.

GARFINKLE. Billy boy, look at me. I weigh a ton. I smoke three packs a day. I walk from here to there I'm out of breath. I can't even steal life insurance. Two years for me is forever. Do what you have to do now. I'm not a long term player.

COLES. I can't do it now. I can't do it till he leaves. If I try I'm out on my ear.

GARFINKLE. *(handing COLES his briefcase)* That's the problem with working for a living.

COLES. Two years is not a long time. I have waited a lifetime for the opportunity.

GARFINKLE. Hey — you got stock, don't you?

COLES. Yes.

GARFINKLE. Fifty, seventy-five thousand, right?

COLES. Sixty.

GARFINKLE. Well, shit, look — want to feel better? *(GARFINKLE taps out stock on his quote machine.)* Before you heard my name your stock was ten. Now it's fourteen and a half. In two months I made you a quarter of a million dollars. Billy boy, the least you can do is smile. Ozzie at the bank, he's sending me flowers. All I'm asking from you is a smile.

COLES. *(Rises, takes his briefcase, and silently moves Center Stage to conference room. He is alone. All else is black.)* Several years ago my doctor told me my right arm is three-fourths of an inch longer than the left. "How do I correct that?" I asked. "Carry the briefcase with your left arm for the next twenty-five years," he said. *(Switches the briefcase to the left arm.)* Charged me a hundred fifty dollars and wished me a good day.

GARFINKLE. *(in the darkness)* Smile, Billy boy, I just made you a quarter of a million dollars.

COLES. How come I like that doctor more than that pig? *(He turns and faces JORGENSON's darkened office.)* Jorgy, it's important.

(Lights up in office as JORGENSON rises to greet him.)

JORGENSON. Come on in. My door is always open. You know that.

(COLES Enters.)

JORGENSON. Welcome home. How was your trip to New York? How's Bill Jr.?

COLES. Fine.

JORGENSON. You must be exhausted. A day in New York is like a month anywhere else. God damned crazy city. Claire do any shopping?

COLES. Some.

JORGENSON. Only some? You got away lucky. Fay used to love to shop there — God rest her soul. Went to this Bergdorf's Department Store, Lord and Taylor's Department Store, but she only bought at this Alexander's Department Store. She was a tight little so and so. Should've married Ozzie.

COLES. She died the year before I got here. Jorgy—

JORGENSON. Last time we were in New York was maybe ... ten, fifteen years ago. We were in a taxicab on that highway coming in from the airport. Traffic? Nobody moved for maybe half an hour. Cars standing still as far as the eye can see. Suddenly some guy behind us went "beep!" Next guy went "beep beep" a little louder. Before you knew it there were these thousands of cars just parked, blaring away, like an orchestra gone mad. Just one giant "beeeeeep." Including my driver. You'd think he'd been thrilled just sitting there on his ass with his foot on the brake listening to that meter go tick tick tick.

COLES. I stopped by at Garfinkle's office.

JORGENSON. Let me just finish. You could hardly hear yourself think. I shout to the driver, "If you ever reach the next exit turn around and take us back to the airport." That's exactly what he did. Fay didn't say a word. Didn't have the nerve. That was the last time we were in New York City ... And you know what was the most amazing thing? It wasn't even rush hour.

COLES. He intends to take over the company.

JORGENSON. Say that again?

COLES. He intends to take over the company.

JORGENSON. He said that?

COLES. He didn't have to. A man with a gun in his hand doesn't have to announce when he pulls the trigger. When you find out you're dead.

JORGENSON. What are you talking about? What gun?

COLES. He now owns eleven percent of the stock.

JORGENSON. I have a million shares. That's twenty-five per cent. If he has a gun — I have a cannon.

COLES. And he's still buying.

JORGENSON. So would you. This is an undervalued company. Give him the credit for recognizing that and putting his money where his mouth is. As it is it's turned out to be a pretty good investment for him. The stock's a lot higher now than when he started buying in.

COLES. Because his buying is moving it up.

JORGENSON. Don't be ridiculous. I'm not saying that's not a factor but it's not the only one. Ozzie told me he bought five thousand shares himself last week. And there are others.

COLES. You don't understand. He's well known. What he does is not a secret. He's called "Larry the Liquidator" on Wall Street. He finds companies worth more dead than alive, gains control and kills them. Then he pockets the proceeds and goes on to the next one. He spelled it out for us right here in this office. It couldn't be any more clear.

JORGENSON. Suppose you're right. What would you like me to do? Last time I looked it was a free country.

COLES. We could do things to protect ourselves.

JORGENSON. Like what?

COLES. We could change our by-laws to call for a two-thirds majority to effect control rather than fifty-one per cent.

JORGENSON. Would that make you feel better?

COLES. Of course it would. At least we'd be fighting back. We wouldn't be rolling over and playing dead.

JORGENSON. Nobody's playing dead! What you propose ... what would it entail?

COLES. Not much. We'd have to change our state of incorporation from Rhode Island to Delaware.

JORGENSON. Delaware? I've never even been to Delaware.

COLES. Neither have I. We needn't be there. We

needn't even visit there. All we'd have to do is hire a local lawyer and get a post office box.

JORGENSON. What would it cost?

COLES. One hundred and seventy-five thousand dollars the first year. Fifty thousand dollars a year thereafter, for local counsel.

JORGENSON. Reclaiming the old stock and issuing the new?

COLES. About two hundred fifty thousand. But that would be a one shot deal.

JORGENSON. For lawyers?

COLES. Primarily.

JORGENSON. Why can't we keep it a Rhode Island company?

COLES. It's easier to get those changes done in Delaware. They're — geared to corporate needs. And we'll show Garfinkle we're not a sitting duck. We intend to fight.

JORGENSON. By running away?

COLES. Running away?

JORGENSON. From Rhode Island to Delaware.

COLES. Nobody's running anywhere. It's a paper transaction.

JORGENSON. I call it running away. This company was founded in Rhode Island. It thrived in Rhode Island. It will remain in Rhode Island.

COLES. It will remain in Rhode Island. All that's moving is the paper.

JORGENSON. And the paper will remain in Rhode Island. Don't talk to me about playing dead. You know me better than that. Our industry is littered with dead bodies. This country is infested with dead bodies. But we're still here. And the lights go on and the telephone rings and orders come in and product goes out and we have money in the bank. And we didn't get there by playing dead.

COLES. At least talk to a lawyer.

JORGENSON. I am not talking to a lawyer. Lawyers are like cab drivers stuck in traffic. They don't do anything — but their meter is always ticking.

COLES. Please ... just think about it.

JORGENSON. I have thought about it. Maybe you ought to think about something. I own twenty-five per cent of this company. The Board owns another ten per cent. The employees' stock ownership plan five per cent. That's forty per cent. How is he going to get control?

COLES. From the sixty left.

JORGENSON. Please. They're long term holders. If they were looking to sell they would've sold when the stock was sixty. I'm sorry, I take your advice most of the time but in this instance you don't know what you're talking about.

COLES. I do know what —

JORGENSON. You are paid to manage this company. Manage it. It's my company. I'll see to it it stays that way, thank you. (COLES pauses a beat, turns and moves Center Stage.)

(Lights out on JORGENSON.)

COLES. "It's my company." Lord of the Manor with the House on the Hill ... How long do you work for something till it's finally yours?

(LIGHTS UP on GARFINKLE in his office. He is watering a small plant on his desk, which appears only in this scene.)

GARFINKLE. How long do you deliver the mail before they give you the post office? Billy boy, they don't give pots of gold to errand boys. They give pensions.

COLES. *(whirling to GARFINKLE)* What?

GARFINKLE. Talk to me. What's happening? How come I don't hear from you? What am I — a creditor?

COLES. I'm busy running a company, Mr. Garfinkle. What can I do for you?

GARFINKLE. Talk to me. Have they broken ground on the Dunkin' Donuts next door?

COLES. I'm afraid not.

GARFINKLE. That's disappointing. Got any more disappointing news? *(long silence)* ... Hellooooo.

COLES. How many shares do you own now, Mr. Garfinkle?

GARFINKLE. You got a one-track mind. That's all you're ever interested in. Aren't you interested in me — my wife — my kids?

COLES. How are you, your wife, your kids?

GARFINKLE. I'm not married. Never was. Don't have any kids. Who would marry me? ... Come to think of it, you might. Shit, with my five hundred thousand shares we're engaged already. Bought the last this morning at fifteen and one-eighth. Ozzie at the bank, he stopped sending me flowers. Now it's plants. Looks like a fucking greenhouse in here. Have you talked to him?

COLES. I don't talk to Ozzie.

GARFINKLE. Not Ozzie. Yorgy.

COLES. What about?

GARFINKLE. Don't act stupid with me, Billy boy. It doesn't become you — not to your fiancée. About restructuring.

COLES. Not yet.

GARFINKLE. You intend to?

COLES. Yes.

GARFINKLE. What are you waiting for?

COLES. The right opportunity.

GARFINKLE. You figure that could occur in my lifetime?

COLES. I don't know, Mr. Garfinkle. I'm not your doctor.

GARFINKLE. You got two weeks.

COLES. Two weeks?

GARFINKLE. Talk to him. Get back to me. Otherwise I'll have to take a ride up there again. Believe me, you don't want to see that happen. I'm less charming the second time.

COLES. Two weeks is unrealistic. I need—

GARFINKLE. Two weeks. Say goodbye.

COLES. Mr. Garfinkle, two weeks—

GARFINKLE. Say goodbye! *(Lights out on COLES. GARFINKLE, breathing hard, turns and yells Offstage.)* Arthur —get the car ready. We're going back to the shitpit of the world. Bring donuts—and oxygen. *(Lights out on GARFINKLE.)*

(Lights up on JORGENSON'S office. COLES and BEA are seated. JORGENSON rises from behind his desk cheerfully.)

JORGENSON. Welcome, Larry, nice to see you again.

(GARFINKLE Enters.)

GARFINKLE. Yumpin' yimminy, Yorgy, was that the sun I almost saw?

JORGENSON. It sure was. Come — look at it again. *(Leads him to window. They stare out.)*

GARFINKLE. Living up here is like living in a limo. You're always looking out from tinted windows.

JORGENSON. Larry, spring is here.

GARFINKLE. Why not? It's been everywhere else.

JORGENSON. Come on. If a beautiful spring day doesn't bring out the sunshine in your soul we'll have to — Bea, c'mon. Let's do it.

BEA. Now?

JORGENSON. Now. *(BEA Exits, excited.)* Wait till you see this, Larry. I haven't even told Bill about it. *(Impatient, yells Offstage.)* C'mon, Bea. We're all waiting.

BEA. *(Offstage)* Hold your horses, Jorgy. I'll be right there.

JORGENSON. Been with me for thirty-seven years. Yelled at me the same way back then.

BEA. *(Offstage)* Ready?

JORGENSON. Ready. Ready. *(BEA Enters pushing a stand-up rack of donuts.)* C'mere — I'll show you how it works. *(He turns handle on top and donuts move up and down like a ferris wheel—different flavored donuts in each rack. Ingenious, actually.)*

BEA. Jorgy designed and built it this morning.

JORGENSON. Willard helped. He's our line foreman. And Kyle at the machine shop lent a hand. Larry, you're looking at a New England Wire and Cable product. Designed and built right here.

BEA. Keep turning.

JORGENSON. *(continuing to turn handle)* This lady drove all the way down to Providence this morning, almost thirty miles — sixty round trip — to get them.

BEA. Closest Dunkin' Donuts I could find. Will you keep turning, Jorgy.

GARFINKLE. With all the pricks in the world I got to do business with a nice guy.

BEA. Look. Raspberry ... toasted coconut.

JORGENSON. It comes apart. You could take it back to New York with you. Keep it in your office. A donut wheel for the donut man.

BEA. Chocolate sprinkles ... chocolate icing ... chocolate fudge ... chocolate cream...

GARFINKLE. *(looking wistfully at the donuts)* How unlucky can you get.

JORGENSON. Know the best part? Know who paid for the donuts? Ozzie at the bank.

GARFINKLE. ... Well, Ozzie ... it's you and me, Babe ... let's get to work.

(Music comes up as stage goes black. Pause a beat. Lights go back up in Conference Room. EVERYONE is there. Time has passed.)

JORGENSON. Larry, do me a favor. I'm a simple man. Restructuring, redeploying, maximizing — don't talk to me in Wall Street. Talk to me in English.

COLES. He wants you to sell the company.

JORGENSON. Is that what it's all about, Larry?

GARFINKLE. *(singing)* "What's it all about, Larry?"

COLES. Tell him. He won't believe me. Tell him.

GARFINKLE. Not the company. Not the company. It's worth bupkus. You're lucky if you get the sixteen dollars a share it's selling at now.

JORGENSON. Then what, Larry? What do you want?

GARFINKLE. I want what every other stockholder wants. I want to make money.

JORGENSON. You are making money.

GARFINKLE. That's right. For all of us. I'm doing my part. Now you do yours.

JORGENSON. Do what? I don't have a printing press out there. I can't simply crank it out.

GARFINKLE. Get rid of the Wire and Cable division. It's a financial cancer. And it's starving out all the other boring things Billy boy runs. Nobody sees them. All they see is the cancer.

JORGENSON. So you want me to sell Wire and Cable.

GARFINKLE. Surgically remove it.

JORGENSON. To who, Mr. Garfinkle? Know anyone interested in buying a surgically removed cancer?

GARFINKLE. I'll find you a buyer.

JORGENSON. Who?

GARFINKLE. What's the difference?

JORGENSON. Who?

GARFINKLE. Some paper shuffling Wall Street types. They'll give you a buck for every four you give them in equipment. I told you that.

COLES. And they'll close this down, and deduct it from their taxes.

GARFINKLE. Easy. Just a paper transaction. Your hands won't even get dirty.

JORGENSON. And what happens to the plant?

GARFINKLE. Gets sold for scrap.

JORGENSON. And the men? And the town?

GARFINKLE. Not your problem. You're not the mayor. You're not a missionary.

JORGENSON. So that's what they mean when they talk about restructuring — maximizing shareholder values?

GARFINKLE. That's what they mean.

JORGENSON. Nice turn of phrase. We used to call it "going out of business."

GARFINKLE. Welcome to the wonderful world of Wall Street.

JORGENSON. Shouldn't surprise me. Those boys down there can't charge millions by going out of business. First they become lawyers and investment bankers — then they restructure.

GARFINKLE. On Wall Street, "Restructuring means never having to say you're sorry." Got it?

JORGENSON. I got it. Now you get it. I understand what you want. Thank you for coming.

GARFINKLE. Yorgy, are you dismissing me?

JORGENSON. I have no time for this. I have a company to run.

GARFINKLE. *(to BEA:)* Sweetheart, pass me a donut. *(She looks at him, uncertain.)* Come on, the chocolate cream.

BEA. Get it yourself.

COLES. Please leave before it becomes unpleasant.

GARFINKLE. Unpleasant? How quaint — how anti-septic — how "New England."

JORGENSON. Get out before I physically throw you out.

GARFINKLE. All right, forget the donut.

JORGENSON. *(rising)* Out!

GARFINKLE. Don't get your bowels in an uproar. We're just doing business.

JORGENSON. Do it somewhere else. You're not welcome here.

GARFINKLE. Now I'm going to tell you something. I don't like the way my company is being run. There is a god damned fire raging here and this whole industry is up in flames. And you call the Fire Department and who shows up? Nobody. Because they're all off in Japan and Singapore and Malaysia and Taiwan and every other shithole place where they're crazy about pollution. And they build factories over there and they stuff them full of little dedicated people who work for twelve cents an hour, ten hours a day, six days a week and then they go home at night and pray for their health so they can come back and do it again tomorrow. And while that god damned inferno is raging you're out front tidying up, mowing the lawn, playing with your putz on my money.

JORGENSON. Now you listen to me. This plant was here before you were born and I promise you — will be here long after you're gone. It's products helped build the roads, bridges and buildings throughout the face of New England. And I will not — do you understand me — will not have it commit suicide and kill these people and this town so you and your cronies can pocket the insurance money.

GARFINKLE. Don't think of it as suicide. Think of it as euthanasia.

JORGENSON. Go back to those other parasites on Wall Street. Tell them to restructure somewhere else. *(GAR-FINKLE moves out of the office toward Center Stage. BEA takes a donut from bin, and hurls it in his direction.)*

BEA. Here's your lousy donut!

JORGENSON. *(Kicks over the bin. The donuts litter the floor.)* Here's all your lousy donuts! *(They laugh. She comes over and they hug.)* God damn it, Bea. It feels good to fight something other than imports for a change. *(Lights out in JORGEN-SON'S office. GARFINKLE is alone Center Stage.)*

GARFINKLE. Geez ... You'd think I was asking them for a loan.

(Lights out. Music plays for several beats as donuts are retrieved from floor.)

KATE. *(in darkness, laughing)* Take over!

(Lights up on KATE alone Onstage as she talks to her unseen mother. KATE is an attractive, sexy woman, about thirty-five.)

KATE. What's so funny? Taking over New England Wire and Cable is like taking over the psychiatric ward at Bellevue. It could be done but who wants to ... Mother, I'm sorry if it was in poor taste. That's who I am ... well, why not take the money and run? You should have retired a long time ago. Now's your chance ... Because I'm busy ... Busy in like having no time.

(Lights up on BEA — in JORGENSON'S office.)

BEA. You can take one day off from Stanley Morgan and fly up here—

KATE. Morgan, Stanley.

BEA. Morgan, Stanley and fly up here and talk to us. Jorgy was always crazy about you.

KATE. I was never crazy about him.

BEA. I did not ask your opinion. I am stating that he would be more at ease speaking to you than some stranger. I expect you to give us a day.

KATE. ... All right. I'm booked solid through the month. One day early next month.

BEA. I'll expect you here tomorrow.

KATE. Tomorrow?

BEA. Tomorrow. Catch the early flight. Come to the plant. We'll all be here.

KATE. *(Sighs, resigned.)* ... Coming, Mother. *(Lights out on BEA.)* Why is it that a grown woman, a lawyer, an executive with a staff of thirty and a budget of eight million plus, responsible for making hundreds of decisions every day, can revert to a spineless infant every time she talks to her mother. *(KATE picks up briefcase and moves to Conference Room.)*

(Lights go up there. BEA, COLES and JORGENSON await.)

KATE. I understand what you said, but I don't understand what you want. Do you want me to help you negotiate a deal with him?

JORGENSON. There is no deal to be made with him.

KATE. Have you tried?

BEA. We want him to go away.

KATE. He's got a half million shares. No one walks away from half a million shares.

COLES. What do you suggest?

KATE. I'm a lawyer. Lawyers don't like to go to court. You never know what can happen there. I suggest you settle.

JORGENSON. Meaning?

KATE. The man is motivated by dollars. Make it worth his while to leave.

COLES. Greenmail. Done all the time. Let's explore it.

JORGENSON. *(rising)* Excuse me. If this discussion continues on this tack I am leaving. We are wasting our time. There is no deal to be made with predators. You kill it or it kills you.

KATE. I was asked what I suggested. It is not my company and it is not my decision. *(She begins to rise as well.)*

BEA. Please Kate, we want to explore our options. Help us defend ourselves.

KATE. *(reluctantly)* All right. Let's say, I'm not at this point recommending anything. Just going over what others in your position have done. "Exploring options," Mother.

(Lights up on GARFINKLE as he views, unseen by them, their meeting.)

GARFINKLE. *(to audience:)* Wait till you hear this.

KATE. Traditionally, first thing, you hire some private investigators, to see what dirt there is. We know some good ones. Hopefully, they'll find something that will make him go away.

GARFINKLE. Aw Kate, you can do better than that.

BEA. Do you think there's a chance? Hasn't he been invesitgated before?

GARFINKLE. *(to audience:)* Investigated? I get sued or subpoenaed every week. I've become a professional witness.

KATE. It's unlikely we'll find anything. He's reasonably well known. I think the S.E.C. got him on a few technical violations.

GARFINKLE. *(to audience:)* That's right, girly. You mug somebody—you're walking the streets the same day. You don't file just one of fourteen hundred bullshit forms they want to put you away for ten years.

COLES. We should do it. We have nothing to lose.

GARFINKLE. *(to audience:)* It's not his money. Us "stuckholders" will pay for it.

JORGENSON. Doesn't sound promising. We have better things to do with our money.

GARFINKLE. The man's got class... or he's cheaper than shit.

KATE. Get the Board to authorize a search for a white knight.

BEA. White knight?

KATE. A protector. A larger company that will buy you out and allow you to do business the way you want. You know, someone to rescue the damsel in distress... a white knight.

JORGENSON. I don't know anyone like that.

BEA. *(to KATE:)* Do you?

GARFINKLE. *(to audience:)* Of course she doesn't. *(Smiles, pats his middle.)* You got to have the stomach for it.

JORGENSON. Next.

KATE. We can formulate a "shark repellent."

BEA. Come again?

KATE. The purpose of a "shark repellent" is to make yourself undesirable to an unwanted suitor, i.e., shark.

BEA. How would that work?

GARFINKLE. *(to audience:)* Listen close. It's an education.

KATE. Take the most attractive part of the company — in this case I assume it's the non-wire and cable divisions — give someone, anyone — the option to buy that part of the business for a song. The option only gets triggered if and when anyone not presently on the Board acquires thirty per cent or more of the company's stock. Garfinkle buys more shares, the option gets triggered. He now owns a lot of shares that are worth considerably less than he paid for them.

JORGENSON. So do we. So do all stockholders.

KATE. That's the risk. The hope is the shark will go elsewhere to feed.

GARFINKLE. *(to audience:)* Ingenious, isn't it? Next.

JORGENSON. Next.

GARFINKLE. Mah *man!*

KATE. We could create a poison pill. It's a form of shark repellent, but one you might find more acceptable. Get the Board to authorize three and a half million shares of preferred stock, one share for each share held by all but Garfinkle. If he gains control of thirty per cent or more issue them for say — a dollar a share.

JORGENSON. A dollar a share!

COLES. What a great idea. We'd make Garfinkle's shares worth less. We'd dilute them.

JORGENSON. We would be diluting ours as well. Book value and earnings per share would be halved.

KATE. Exactly. Once you swallow the poison pill you're no longer desirable. But you can still keep your businesses. To most everyone nothing has changed.

GARFINKLE. *(to audience)* Except the stuckholder. People get paid big money — honored people — pillars of the community — to sit and dream this shit up. You know what I said when I first heard it?

JORGENSON. That's legal?

GARFINKLE. *(to audience:)* That's what I said.

KATE. So far.

GARFINKLE. *(to audience:)* Would you believe it?

KATE. It's not new. I can give you a list of companies — household names — that have it in their corporate by-laws.

GARFINKLE. *(to audience:)* If you or me tried it they'd have us committed.

JORGENSON. How much would your firm charge for taking us on?

KATE. I don't know. That's not my department.

JORGENSON. Rough guess?

KATE. It would depend on how involved it got. If we were able to work it out peacefully and quickly — a million. Maybe two. If it turned out to be war it could go to ten, twenty times that.

JORGENSON. Kate, your mother is the only assistant I ever had. She is also the best friend I ever had. I remember clearly the day you were born. The whole plant shut down a full afternon while we had birthday cake and celebrated. This whole plant...

BEA. Jorgy, please.

JORGENSON. And it is out of respect for that lady that I don't have you bodily thrown out of this office.

GARFINKLE. Bravo, Yorgy!

KATE. I'm sorry you feel that way. I'm only telling you how corporations under attack defend themselves. Don't blame the messenger for the message.

JORGENSON. The messenger, as I hear it, is saying pay him off or self-destruct. Either way, pay me my fee.

KATE. It is not my fee. Unfortunately, I'm only an employee. *(picking up her briefcase to leave)* I'm sorry we wasted each other's time.

JORGENSON. Have your firm send me a bill. That way only our time will have been wasted. I trust it'll be for something less than a million dollars.

KATE. It will. This one is on the house. And as long as it's my nickel I want to tell you something. You, as they say on the street, are "in play." Garfinkle put you there. And now, right this second, all over the country there sit all kinds of boring, dull little men, hunched over their IBM PC's buried under mountains of 13-D filings, looking for an edge to make a buck. And some of their little mini computers have already noticed an obscure over the counter stock with a sixty per cent move in the last two months. "What's this? How come? What's going on?" they mutter. And then they notice Garfinkle's 13-D and his half million shares, and they don't have to know diddly-doo about wire and cable. They know Garfinkle and they ride the coattails. Congratulations. You're now "in play" in the big leagues where the game is called hardball and winner takes all. So if you want to play Mr. High and Mighty, Mr. Principled, Mr. Roberts Rule of Order, better go to work for the Peace Corps where you'll be appreciated because you won't have any company left here to run. *(Begins to Exit, turns.)* And the shame of it is I would be perfect for this deal. Garfinkle is a blatant sexist. I love blatant sexists. They're my meat. But I wouldn't work for you if you begged me. I like being associated with winners.

(Lights out in Conference Room.)

GARFINKLE. *(fanning himself)* Phew ... some piece of work.

(Lights out on GARFINKLE.)

BEA. How dare you talk to him that way.

KATE. Will you stop defending him. He is making the wrong decision. He will lose this company.

BEA. He is making the right decision. We will not lose this company.

KATE. We!? Since when is it "we"? He loses this company he walks away with millions. You walk away with memories.

BEA. Don't you worry about me. I'm well provided for.

KATE. "Well provided for." You have running water you think you're well provided for.

BEA. Why are we talking about my finances? What is

this all about?

KATE. Anger. About thirty five years worth.

BEA. At whom?

KATE. At him. And you. And this god awful company. It's your life. It always was. When he was happy you were ecstatic. When he was depressed you were distraught. When she died you almost moved in. It was the talk of the town. With Dad keeping the dinner warm.

BEA. I loved him.

KATE. You were married, Mother.

BEA. Listen to me, Kate. In a life filled with rumors and gossip and sideways glances — I apologized to no one. Don't expect it of me now. You won't get it. You were asked here as our attorney, not our judge. If you can't handle the position — leave.

KATE. Why in God's name did you ever marry Dad?

BEA. I was nineteen. He asked. I thought I loved him. Until one day, thank God, I walked through that door. And there stood the most beautiful, scared young man I had ever seen. Had on blue jeans and a red flannel shirt with the sleeves rolled up. Said he just became President. I remember thinking, "How peculiar for a President. This company'll never last." And then the magic words: "How about it, Miss? I'm ready to take a chance with you. Ready to take one with me?" *(Turns to KATE.)* Sometimes life presents us with very limited choices.

KATE. I know.

BEA. Like now.

KATE. I don't believe you.

BEA. He trusts you. Don't make us deal with strangers

in three piece suits. Maybe we can't play the game the way you want us to — help us play our game the best we can.

KATE. Oh Mother, don't you think I want to. Going up against Garfinkle, he's the best. And I'm as good as he is. It's the career opportunity of a lifetime.

BEA. So?

KATE. So I said I wouldn't. Even if he begged me.

BEA. He's not. I am. *(KATE pauses a beat, picks up her briefcase and crosses to her mother on the way to JORGENSON'S office. Looks back.)*

KATE. Well c'mon. *(BEA moves to her and they begin their Exit.)*

BEA. And you'll do something about those fees. They're horrendous.

KATE. Mom. Don't push it. *(They Exit.)*

(Lights up on GARFINKLE.)

GARFINKLE. *(to audience:)* You know what kills me? I've done maybe seven — eight deals like this. Know who I negotiate with? Skinny little joggers with contact lenses all stinking from the same after shave. Don't believe me? Ever seen an arbitrageur? Ugliest people on the face of the earth. They won't use her. You'll see. I never luck out with a broad like that. Excuse me, woman like that. I've been accused of being a "womanizer." That's someone who likes broads. I remember when that used to be a good thing ... Although when you cut through the "Woman's Lib" bullshit all it really means is you can't call them "sweetheart" and "darling" unless you're schtuping them ... then you can't call them anything else. *(Sits behind his desk, smiles.)* I can live with that.

(KATE Enters his office. Hands him her business card.)

KATE. That's me. We're the investment banker for New England Wire and Cable.

GARFINKLE. *(looking at card)* What are you — a fucking lawyer?

KATE. *(smiling)* Depends on who I'm with.

GARFINKLE. *(Rises — opens arms — beams.)* Welcome to my life!

KATE. All those cubby holes have lawyers in them?

GARFINKLE. Mostly. *(She gives him a sad look.)* It's not as bad as you think. I don't have to talk to them. I just have to pay them.

KATE. You don't talk to them?

GARFINKLE. Talk to them? I'd rather talk to my mother. I write to them. *(Takes top sheet from pile on desk. Writes.)* "Fuck ... them." *(Looks up at KATE.)* Sue. *(Picks up the next sheet. Writes.)* "Trouble." *(Looks up at KATE.)* Settle. *(Picks up the next sheet, writes.)* "They're ... morons." *(Looks up at KATE.)* Let them sue. Don't give them a quarter. *(KATE laughs.)* See? Nothing to it. Sue. Settle. Defend. Which one are you?

KATE. I came to talk.

GARFINKLE. Now that's trouble. Lawyers want to talk, it's nothing but trouble. Who are you? How come I never heard of you?

KATE. They generally keep me locked away at bond closings, due diligence meetings, good stuff like that.

GARFINKLE. Life in the fast lane.

KATE. I'm not complaining. They pay well. I meet a lot of people. *(GARFINKLE yawns.)* Well ... it's true. They don't have your ... something.

GARFINKLE. *(opening desk drawer)* Want a donut?

KATE. No thanks.

GARFINKLE. Why not — you a health food freak?

KATE. No. Just not hungry.

GARFINKLE. *(incredulous)* You have to be hungry to have a donut?

KATE. ... you don't?

GARFINKLE. Are you shitting me? In all my life I never heard of such a thing. Have to be hungry? Why? It don't taste better that way.

KATE. How would you know?

GARFINKLE. My luck. A broad with a mouth.

KATE. Show me a broad worth knowing who doesn't have one.

GARFINKLE. I like you. Can you tell?

KATE. Not yet.

GARFINKLE. Hang in. You will.

KATE. That's what I came to see you about. I need a month to hang in.

GARFINKLE. Get lost.

KATE. I just got involved. I need time to get everybody's act together.

GARFINKLE. My act is together.

KATE. If you give me some time I think we can work something out.

GARFINKLE. Settle?

KATE. Work something out.

GARFINKLE. I only settle when I'm in trouble.

KATE. Or when it makes sense.

GARFINKLE. It only makes sense when I'm in trouble.

KATE. If you'd prefer we'll go to court, get an injunction, have a fight, all kinds of allegations, cost them, cost you, and for what?

GARFINKLE. I live in court. You got to do better than that.

KATE. ... I won't love you anymore.

GARFINKLE. ... You got two weeks.

KATE. Standstill agreement.

GARFINKLE. Both sides.

KATE. No more buying.

GARFINKLE. Two weeks.

KATE. Thank you. *(She begins to Exit.)*

GARFINKLE. Now let's talk about what I want to talk about.

KATE. What's that?

GARFINKLE. Your legs ... your ass ... your tits—

KATE. Garfinkle, sit. *(beat)* Sit!! *(He sits.)* Listen close. I don't want to repeat this. You listening? Now take your right hand out of that donut drawer and put it between your legs. *(He looks at her, uncertain.)* Come on. They visit each other all the time. *(He laughs ... a little nervously.)*

GARFINKLE. ... Can't.

KATE. Why?

GARFINKLE. I'm a lefty. *(Switches hands. Fumbles a bit, but does it.)*

KATE. Good. Now look directly down at the little guy and say — "You must behave yourself when you're in the presence of a lady." *(GARFINKLE laughs.)* Garfinkle, if you don't say exactly that, right now, I'm resigning from this case. You'll deal with the Morgan Stanley "B" team. They think arbitrageurs are fun. *(He remains motionless. She rises, begins to Exit.)*

GARFINKLE. All right. All right.

KATE. "You must behave yourself when you're in the presence of a lady."

GARFINKLE. ... You must — *(KATE motions him to put his chin on chest. He does.)* "You must behave yourself when you're in the presence of a lady."

KATE. See, not so hard. *(He does a double take to his crotch as she rises to Exit.)* Hey, Garfinkle, what kind of donuts you got in that drawer?

GARFINKLE. The good kind.

KATE. Toss one over. *(He reaches into drawer.)* With the right hand. *(He switches hands and tosses one over. She catches it.)* See you in two weeks. *(She Exits. He rises, takes a step or two Downstage, his voice filled with wonder.)*

GARFINKLE. ... I think I'm falling in love ... *(Lights out on GARFINKLE — up on KATE as she munches donut.)*

KATE. The man does have ... a certain undeniable ... charm.

(Lights up in Conference Room. JORGENSON, COLES and BEA await.)

BEA. Charm? He has as much charm as a beached whale.

(KATE enters office.)

KATE. Don't knock it. It bought us two weeks.

JORGENSON. For what?

KATE. For getting our act together.

JORGENSON. What did it cost?

KATE. A donut

COLES. Where do we go from here?

KATE. *(to JORGENSON:)* Have you reconsidered the defenses we spoke about?

JORGENSON. We won't do that.

KATE. Can I threaten it?

JORGENSON. I don't make threats I won't fulfill.

KATE. It's probably too late in the game for that anyway. Here's what you can do. Get the Board together. Authorize the purchase of as many shares as you can afford. Do it right away.

JORGENSON. The dollars we have are our safety net. Most of it is earmarked for future expansion.

KATE. Then borrow the money.

COLES. We have excellent credit. There's a dozen banks happy to lend us the money. It would be no problem.

JORGENSON. It's never a problem borrowing money. It's only a problem paying it back. *(to KATE:)* What would that do?

KATE. Three things. One: For every share you aquire it's one less Garfinkle can get. Two, and more important, you'll drive the price of the stock up. Eighteen sounds terrific when the stock is ten. Twenty is not so terrific when the stock is eighteen. The more it costs the more negotiable he becomes. Get the stock up.

JORGENSON. I understand what you're saying. I'm not sure I want to do that. We've been debt free since the

Depression. It's what's permitted us to survive.

KATE. And it's that gorgeous balance sheet that also makes you so attractive — which is the third reason to buy the shares.

JORGENSON. What a strange new world. A strong, liquid balance sheet is no longer an asset. It's a liability.

KATE. Next, get a letter out to shareholders. Tell them how great business is and how wonderful the future looks. Tell them how pleased you are that the investment community is finally beginning to recognize, in some small way, the real worth of the company. Thank them for their loyalty and support. Talk to as many of the larger shareholders as you can, personally. Under no circumstances mention any potential takeover.

BEA. I'll compile a list of everyone with more than five thousand shares.

JORGENSON. I don't need a list. I know who they are.

KATE. You have any political clout?

BEA. We're friendly with the Mayor and City Council.

KATE. Forget them. Too small. Do you have a relationship with the Governor?

BEA. Are you kidding? He's a Democrat.

KATE. That's OK. I'll set it up from New York. We'll get some of our legislative people up here to talk to him. Prepare a statistical analysis of your dollar contribution to the local economy: jobs, payroll, taxes, etc. Make it as complete as possible.

COLES. You'll have it Monday.

KATE. Maybe we can get some anti-takeover legislation passed — quickly.

COLES. I don't mean to be crass ... but ... shouldn't we deal with something commonly called ... "golden parachutes"?

BEA. Golden parachutes?

KATE. You're premature. Don't muddy the water. We'll have time for that later.

JORGENSON. I think you've given us enough to tackle for the moment. We still have a business to run.

KATE. I agree. The important thing for now is to get the stock up. I'll coordinate everything else. *(Begins to Exit.)*

JORGENSON. Before you go, will you answer the question I asked you earlier?

KATE. What's that?

JORGENSON. Why did he give us two weeks? What did it cost?

KATE. *(smiling)* ... I told you — A donut. Chocolate fudge with sprinkles. *(KATE Exits. JORGENSON moves Center Stage. Lights go out in his office.)*

JORGENSON. Donut my ass. Garfinkle would never give two weeks. He'd sell them.

BEA. Jorgy, what the hell is a "golden parachute"? *(Lights go out on JORGENSON and BEA as they Exit.)*

(KATE screams in the darkness.)

KATE. You son-of-a-bitch! You god damned son-of-a-bitch!

(Lights up in GARFINKLE'S office. KATE Enters. Flings papers at him.)

KATE. God damned hypocrite liar!

GARFINKLE. But, sweetie pie, but, honey lamb—

KATE. We had an agreement. You gave me your word.

GARFINKLE. But, baby poo—

KATE. Stop that. You lied to me.

GARFINKLE. Me?

KATE. We had a standstill. No more buying.

GARFINKLE. So?

KATE. So? What's this tender to buy New England Wire and Cable at twenty dollars a share all about?

GARFINKLE. Not me.

KATE. I bet. *(Picks up papers.)* OPM holdings — you know nothing about it?

GARFINKLE. OPM? Not a lot to know.

KATE. I'm sure ... Where's the money coming from — junk bonds?

GARFINKLE. Through Drexel. Give them fifteen per cent plus a fee and they'll get you the bucks to buy a slag heap in Mound City, Missouri.

KATE. Why did you have to lie to me? You embarrassed me with my firm. You embarrassed me with my clients.

GARFINKLE. *(Slams his hand on desk. The ferocity of the blow startles KATE.)* Enough! Who am I dealing with here — Mother Teresa? Don't come on so god damned holy with me, girly. You think I'm a fool — I sit here and twiddle my thumbs while you drive the price of the stock up?

KATE. I did no such thing.

GARFINKLE. You're full of shit. All the buying was coming from some cock-a-mamie little brokerage firm in Rhode Island.

KATE. I know nothing about it.

GARFINKLE. Give me a break, will you? That cheapskate is so tight he won't put paint on the walls. The only way he'd be paying seventeen for his stock is if someone stood behind him with a cattle prod. I got as good an imagination as most but I tell you it's tough picturing Mother Teresa with a cross in one hand and a cattle prod in the other. *(KATE begins to leave.)* Don't go, Katie. I'm not through. You want to play the game — let's play. Only I don't watch while you do "holier than thou." That's not the way this game is gonna get played.

KATE. Is that what it is for you, a game?

GARFINKLE. God damned right. The best game in the world.

KATE. You're playing Monopoly with people's lives here.

GARFINKLE. I'm doing them a favor. I'm making them money. I thought that's what they were in business for.

KATE. I know this might be difficult for you to believe — for some people business means more than making money. They don't know how to play your game.

GARFINKLE. I'll teach them. It's easy. You make as much as you can for as long as you can.

KATE. And then what?

GARFINKLE. And then what? Whoever has the most when he dies — wins.

KATE. Goodbye, Garfinkle.

GARFINKLE. Aw Katie, don't leave. We haven't spoken about your thighs, your nipples, your—

KATE. See you in court.

GARFINKLE. At least have a donut.

KATE. Stuff it.

GARFINKLE. *(Downstage Right)* You didn't have to leave. I'm not mad at you. Lying to protect your client is just doing your job good.

KATE. Round One to the fat man. It ain't over till it's over, fat man.

GARFINKLE. And you didn't even ask me what OPM stands for. *(A short burst of MUSIC. Smiling.)* "Other People's Money." *(Another short burst of MUSIC, a cymbal-like grace-note.)*

BLACKOUT

ACT II

MUSIC plays—ending with a champagne "Pop." Lights come up
on KATE with champagne bottle in hand in Conference
Room. JORGENSON, COLES and BEA are standing
expectantly.

KATE. To Judge Pollard.

BEA. Judge Jim Pollard? For what?

KATE. For granting us an injunction preventing Garfinkle from buying more shares. *(They cheer, delighted.)*

COLES. A permanent injunction?

KATE. No. Pending the results of a suit we filed in Washington with the S.E.C. But since our Annual Meeting is in five weeks, for the purposes of taking control at that time, you could consider it permanent.

COLES. No more buying?

KATE. No more buying. He'll look to overturn it but he doesn't have time.

JORGENSON. Not with Jim Pollard presiding. Used to play football together in high school. Slowest son of a bitch on the team.

KATE. Didn't move slowly here. Granted us the injunction in two hours.

GARFINKLE. *(Sings.)* "Territory folks should stick together."

KATE. Our legislative people met yesterday with the Governor and his Secretary of Commerce to discuss immediate anti-takeover legislation. They seem, I am told, very sympathetic.

GARFINKLE. *(Sings.)* "Territory folks should all be pals."

KATE. I want to organize bus trips to the state capitol. Get the workers, management, local politicians, everyone in town up there to see the legislators. And demonstrate, demonstrate, demonstrate.

GARFINKLE. *(Sings.)* "Cowboys dance with the farmer's daughters."

KATE. I want to see babies. I want to see balloons. I want to see "Save Our Town, Save Our Future" posters hung from every school, church, bank and whorehouse in this city. I want visibility. I want prayer meetings. I want pressure!

GARFINKLE. *(Sings.)* "Farmers dance with the rancher's gals!" *(Lights fade in Conference Room. KATE moves Center Stage.)*

KATE. God save me ... I love this!

(Lights up in GARFINKLE'S office as he berates his unseen staff. KATE looks on in amusement.)

GARFINKLE. Seventeen lawyers on my payroll. Three god damned law firms on retainer. And all of you together ain't worth one broad wet behind the ears. Some crew — you managed to work it out so in a free market in a free country I can't buy some shit-ass stock that every other asshole can buy. Congratulations. You know what? You—all of you—are destroying the capitalist system. And you know what happens when capitalism is destroyed, don't you? The Communists take over. And you know the one good thing that happens when the Commies take over? The first thing they do, they kill all the lawyers. And if they miss any of you— I'll do it myself. *(KATE, moving into his office, applauds.)* You liked it?

KATE. Loved it.

GARFINKLE. The Wall Street version of "Let's win one for the Gipper."

KATE. It was wonderful. It's a shame Judge Pollard couldn't hear you.

GARFINKLE. Stop gloating. It doesn't become you. What do you want?

KATE. A donut.

GARFINKLE. *(mimicking her)* It's too early to be hungry.

KATE. *(mimicking him)* You have to be hungry to have a donut?

GARFINKLE. *(tossing her a donut)* I see gloating is good for the appetite.

KATE. Who would know better than you.

GARFINKLE. My luck. I meet a broad ... sweet, nice, Irish. In two weeks she turns into Don Rickles. *(KATE laughs.)* I like it when you laugh. You laugh nice.

KATE. You have the most incredible sense of humor. You make me laugh.

GARFINKLE. Uh-oh. Here it comes. I'm in trouble.

KATE. Let's be friends. Let's work it out. Let's settle.

GARFINKLE. You've been eating too many donuts.

KATE. You only settle when you're in trouble. I thought I heard, "I'm in trouble."

GARFINKLE. Only with you. You're wet behind the ears.

I want you wet between your legs. *(KATE chokes on her donut.)* Aha — gotcha. *(She nods, still choking.)* Nice to see a girl blush nowadays. *(He moves behind her, gently and awkwardly patting her back as one would a child.)*

KATE. ... Not blushing ... choking.

GARFINKLE. ... Are you all right? *(She nods.)* Good. I don't want you to sue Dunkin' Donuts. The only thing better than their donuts is their stock.

KATE. Now that you almost killed me, can we talk?

GARFINKLE. Talk. I'm listening. Just don't die on me.

KATE. What do you want to go away?

GARFINKLE. ... What do you mean?

KATE. What number do we buy you out at? *(GARFINKLE, feigning horror, pretends to draw drapes, check for bugs, etc.)* What are you doing?

GARFINKLE. Greenmail! Are you offering me greenmail?

KATE. Will you stop it!

GARFINKLE. Are you?

KATE. Stop acting like it's new to you. You've done it three times in the past.

GARFINKLE. I've done shit in the past. I don't play that way. It was never my idea. *(talking into her briefcase)* And I want the record to show it's not in this case either.

KATE. Why are you so uptight? It's not illegal.

GARFINKLE. No, it's not. It's immoral. That distinction has no relevance for you lawyers — but it matters to me.

KATE. For someone who has nothing nice to say about

lawyers you certainly have enough of them around.

GARFINKLE. You have to. They're like nuclear warheads. They have theirs so you need yours — but once you use them they fuck everything up. They're only good in their silos.

KATE. *(Laughs.)* I'll have to remember that.

GARFINKLE. Let me ask you something? You have authorization to offer me greenmail? ... Bet your ass you don't. The others didn't either. It only comes from the lawyers. It's a lawyer's scheme. Everybody walks out happy. I get paid off. You get paid off. Yorgy keeps his company. Billy boy keeps his inheritance. The employees keep their jobs. Everyone comes out.

KATE. Sounds pretty good to me.

GARFINKLE. Except the stuckholders. Their stock falls out of bed. They won't know what hit them.

KATE. I don't believe this. We better stop hanging out together. I turn into Don Rickles and you turn into Albert Schweitzer.

GARFINKLE. Not Albert Schweitzer — Robin Hood. I'm a modern-day Robin Hood. I take from the rich and give to the middle-class. *(KATE laughs derisively.)* Well ... upper middle-class.

KATE. Can we be serious now?

GARFINKLE. I am serious. I really believe that ... So what's your number?

KATE. The stock is eighteen. We'll buy it back at eighteen.

GARFINKLE. First you laugh at me and then you insult me.

KATE. Why? Who else you know would buy a million

shares of New England Wire and Cable at eighteen?

GARFINKLE. Me. I'll pay twenty for them.

KATE. You can't. You got trouble.

GARFINKLE. No trouble. Just delay.

KATE. I could maybe ... get them to stretch to twenty.

GARFINKLE. Now why would I sell you something at the same price I was willing to pay for it?

KATE. Your average cost was thirteen. Thirteen from twenty, times a million, isn't a bad day's pay on one little deal.

GARFINKLE. I'm not interested in seven million. I'm interested in value. The value here is no secret. I spelled it out for them. I was being conservative.

KATE. Spell it out for me. What's the number?

GARFINKLE. Twenty-five.

KATE. Impossible.

GARFINKLE. What's impossible — It's worth it or they'll pay it?

KATE. Both. That stock hasn't seen twenty-five in ten years.

GARFINKLE. You want history? That stock was once sixty. I was once skinny ... well, skinnier.

KATE. Take twenty.

GARFINKLE. Take a walk. Twenty-five is my number. And that is a favor.

KATE. I can't deliver that.

GARFINKLE. I know. Let's talk about something nice. Let's talk about your eyes.

KATE. *(getting up to leave)* I really thought we could work something out.

GARFINKLE. We can't. You're too far away.

KATE. You could lose it all.

GARFINKLE. I could. That's why so few of us have the balls to play the game.

KATE. Thanks for the donut.

GARFINKLE. Don't be depressed. You're in a tough place. Go fight your fight. It's not personal — it's principle. Hey, no matter what — it's better than working at the post office.

KATE. *(softly)* Oh yeah ... It's better than the post office. *(She smiles sadly and Exits. He is alone.)*

GARFINKLE. A lot better than the post office. It's the best there is. Like in the old westerns, didn't everyone want to be a gunslinger? Didn't everyone want to be Butch Cassidy and the James Boys? There's just a few of us — us modern-day gunslingers. There's T. Boone and the Bass Brothers out of Texas. Irwin Jacobs out of Minneapolis. Would you believe a gunslinger named Irwin Jacobs? There's the Belzberg Boys up north in Canada. And here in New York we got Saul Steinberg and Ronald Perlman and Carl Icahn. *(Places his hand on his heart.)* Out of respect for the stupid a moment of silence for our gunned-down colleague Ivan Boesky. *(with a big smile)* It's assholes like him that give assholes like us a bad name. And last, but not least, Garfinkle from the wilds of the Bronx. But instead of galloping in with a six gun a-blazing in each hand, we're driven in, escorted by a herd of lawyers and investment bankers, waving our 13-D filings in one hand and our limited partnerships in the other. But they quake just as hard. And they wind up just as dead. And it's legal. And it's exciting. And it's fun.

(Moves to desk.) And the money ain't bad either. *(Sits at desk.)* And every so often, every once in a while, we even wind up with the girl. *(Begins looking at papers on desk. Looks up.)* It's a nice business.

(As he works quietly for a beat, we hear KATE shouting Offstage.)

KATE. *(Offstage)* What? What are you so hysterical about — interrupting my meeting.

(She Enters his office.)

KATE. What the hell is so important? You having a stroke — a nervous breakdown?

GARFINKLE. Just taking care of business.

KATE. You're worse than my mother.

GARFINKLE. Please. I know we're on different sides here—

KATE. I'm busy. What's so important? What do you want?

GARFINKLE. I feel bad about our last meeting. You left, you looked so depressed. I want us to be friends. I want us to end our dispute. I have two propositions. I'll give them to you in my order of preference. *(She sits.)* Sure. If I was having a stroke you'd tell me to dial 911. — Now you're ready to spend the afternoon. How about the evening?

KATE. Proposition number one?

GARFINKLE. We leave here, right now, and go to my place where we make wild passionate love for the rest of the afternoon.

KATE. Number two?

GARFINKLE. I'm not finished. The first one who comes, loses.

KATE. *(A beat)* Loses what?

GARFINKLE. The deal. I come first I sell you back my shares at cost. I slink away never to be seen or heard from again. You come first, you tender all your shares to me at twenty.

KATE. You're serious?

GARFINKLE. Well. — I don't slink. Big men don't slink. I ... saunter away.

KATE. How do you suggest we write this up for the proxy statement?

GARFINKLE. Delicately. Under the heading, "easy come, easy go."

KATE. The garment center is too classy for you.

GARFINKLE. Come on, what do you got to lose — your virginity? I could lose millions.

KATE. You've thought of everything!

GARFINKLE. Not everything. What happens if we come together?

KATE. We call and make sure your life insurance premiums are paid. *(KATE moves out of office to Center Stage.)*

GARFINKLE. Hey, premiums are paid. *(Lights out on GARFINKLE. KATE is alone.)*

KATE. You think he was serious? So help me, I don't know. On the one hand if he was serious ... *(She laughs.)* We would have made Wall Street history ... maybe. *(moving to Conference Room)* On the other hand, proposition number two is something to talk about.

(Lights up in Conference Room. BEA, COLES and JORGENSON excitedly greet KATE as she Enters.)

KATE. Don't get excited. Don't break out the champagne. He gave me two propositions. Here's the one worth talking about. In as much as Judge Pollard will not lift his injunction and in as much as his money is tied up, and, if I may say so, in as much as your lawyer can be very persuasive, he's agreeable to swap you his shares for the Wire and Cable division.

BEA. ...What?

KATE. He owns a million shares. He gives them to us. We give him the Wire and Cable division.

COLES. Makes sense. It costs him thirteen million for something he'll sell for thirty — thirty-five million.

JORGENSON. *(trying to control himself)* What are the alternatives?

KATE. Don't dismiss it so quickly. On Wall Street this is known as "restructuring." Look what happens. The losses at Wire and Cable disappear. The earnings of the other divisions surface. Your stock skyrockets.

JORGENSON. What are the alternatives?

KATE. Better yet, you get back his million shares you absolutely control this company. It's yours. No one can take it away.

JORGENSON. I'm asking you for the last—

KATE. I can't play with him in the courts forever. Ultimately he gets the injunction withdrawn, buys more shares ... don't you understand?

BEA. We're not stupid — we understand. What are the alternatives!

KATE. Greenmail. Poison pills. Restructuring. You choose. I have given you the alternatives.

JORGENSON. You've given me nothing but different ways to kill myself.

COLES. Jorgy, this idea works. We're rid of the losses. We're in total control. Our stock doubles.

JORGENSON. To hell with the price of our stock. I will not do Garfinkle's dirty work for him.

KATE. I'm pleading with you. I'm imploring you.

JORGENSON. Damn it, Kate, — these men haven't had an increase for three years. My salary is half what it was. Dividends are half what they were. Everybody's sacrificed. And it's working. No — No, I won't. I will not kill these people and this town to enrich the man who is trying to destroy me.

KATE. You're a fool. You're a neanderthal. You deserve to lose this company!

BEA. Stop that. This is not a chess game. It's not simply a matter of tactics. What's the matter with you? This used to be your home. This is family.

KATE. Family!?

BEA. Yes. The kids you went to school with earn their livings at this plant. Family.

KATE. Oh good God. Ok let's talk about family. Let's start with Dad. Let's start with his dreams and his family.

BEA. Your father is dead, Kate. But we're not dead. And this plant is not dead. And our dreams aren't over. And they'll never end with greenmail and poison pills.

KATE. Stop talking dreams. Look at the reality.

BEA. I am. I don't like what I see. It scares me. Who are you Kate? Whatever happened to that brave young girl who set out to do battle to heal all the world's ills? *(distraught)* Whatever happened to my baby? *(Jorgenson moves to BEA. With his arm around her shoulder, he begins ushering her off.)*

JORGENSON. Please.

BEA. What are you doing? She is my daughter. This is my fight.

JORGENSON. This is our company. This is my fight, too. I won't embarrass you. Promise. *(BEA reluctantly Exits. KATE begins to leave.)* Hold on a minute ... What do you want of me Kate? Want me to say "I'm sorry?" For what? For loving your Mother? I'm not. Look, we are fighting for our lives — here and now ... Why are we even talking about this?

KATE. Because it still hurts.

JORGENSON. Well, what do we do now? Go over it — resolve thirty some odd years of hurt in the next fifteen minutes? Is that what you expect?

KATE. No I don't. But I'll tell you what I do expect. I expect not to be lectured to about "family" by my mother and not be abused by you.

JORGENSON. Abused?

KATE. I turned my life upside down to come up here to help you out. I don't even get to take off my jacket and you're ready to have me "bodily thrown out of your office." Well I'll make it easy for you. I'll leave. *(She turns to Exit.)*

JORGENSON. Well go ahead then and leave. You're a lousy lawyer anyway.

KATE. *(returning)* Lousy lawyer!? I want to tell you something. I'm a god damned good lawyer. You are a lousy client. You say "No" to everything. You say "No" to what ninety nine per cent of other corporations say "Yes" to. If this was any other outfit they'd put a statue out there in the yard of the woman that saved this company.

JORGENSON. Saved this company? You're not looking to save this company. You're looking to save your own ass.

KATE. ...What?

JORGENSON. Being beaten by Garfinkle wouldn't look so good on your resume, would it? Damn it Kate — you want to win so badly, you don't even know what this fight is all about!

KATE. Oh yes I do. It's about your incredible — pigheadedness.

JORGENSON. OK. Sure it is. But it's more than that. It's also about the 1200 men who work here and their families. Let's ask them if you're trying to "save this company."

KATE. Why ask them? They're not stockholders.

JORGENSON. Does that mean they don't matter?

KATE. ... OK ... Look. They matter. They matter. Nothing gets resolved but everything matters.

JORGENSON. What matters most is that we stop fighting about what I won't do and let's start fighting about what I will do.

KATE. OK. Here's my problem. I'm a good lawyer. I'm a lousy mindreader. What will you do?

JORGENSON. I'll leave it up to the stockholders. (KATE laughs in exasperation.)

KATE. You will leave it up to the stockholders?

JORGENSON. They haven't let me down yet.

KATE. They haven't met Garfinkle yet.

JORGENSON. I don't have a choice. I do — not —

have a choice I can live with.

KATE. Oh, why couldn't you be an asshole like everybody else?

JORGENSON. I'm sorry. I thought I was doing my best.

KATE. OK — look. This 40% ... This faithful 40% ... Can you absolutely count on them?

JORGENSON. Absolutely. Come on, let's kick his ass all the way back to Wall Street.

KATE. Jorgy, if I play Garfinkle right. If I massage that ego just right, this could work. *(KATE and JORGENSON cross into his office.)*

(COLES Enters alone, addresses audience.)

COLES. It didn't seem the appropriate time to ask: "And what happens to me if we lose?" It never seemed the appropriate time to ask that. When you spend your life managing a business you're trained to think in contingencies. What happens if sales don't meet expectations? What happens if costs go up — the economy down? What happens if...

So ... later that afternoon, with a lump in my throat, I asked, "What happens to me if we lose? I deserve 'a golden parachute.' Managements with far worse records than mine routinely give themselves at least five years pay. It's done all the time. And it wouldn't cost you a thing." ... Know what he said?

JORGENSON. *(in his darkened office)* Up here we don't plan the funeral until someone dies.

COLES. Isn't that something? *(COLES Exits.)*

(Lights up in JORGENSON'S office. KATE is preparing to leave.)

JORGENSON. So ... You think he'll go for it?

KATE. ... I don't know.

JORGENSON. You can do it. Use some of that home grown New England charm. Talk nice. Smile sweet. You'll get him.

KATE. Don't go away. *(She turns to GARFINKLE'S darkened office.)* Hey Garfinkle! Rumor has it you got balls.

(Lights go up on GARFINKLE in his office.)

GARFINKLE. I've been trying to show you for weeks.

KATE. *(moving into Conference Room area)* Show me now. Let's leave it up to the stockholders. We'll let you run your own slate of directors at the Annual Meeting. You get 51% of the votes, it's your company. You buy everybody out at twenty. You don't get the votes, you sell us back your shares at thirteen. You slink away, never to be seen or heard from again ... What do you say, Garfinkle? Hardball. Winner takes all.

GARFINKLE. Is that what you want?

KATE. A lot.

GARFINKLE. I don't know. It's a tough proposition. You control 40% of the votes going in.

KATE. What do you got to lose? On a worst case basis

you come out even. It only cost you thirteen.

GARFINKLE. I don't know. It's gonna be close.

KATE. Robin Hood makes the deal.

GARFINKLE. ... Yeah. Do it. *(Lights out on GARFINKLE'S office.)*

(KATE turns to JORGENSON'S office. Lights come up. BEA and JORGENSON are present.)

KATE. Done. *(She moves to Exit.)*

JORGENSON. Hold on. Where are you going?

KATE. The airport.

JORGENSON. I'll give you a lift.

KATE. Don't bother.

JORGENSON. At least let me tell you how great you did.

KATE. We'll see at the Annual Meeting.

BEA. I know this wasn't your preference. Thanks for sticking your neck out. How does it feel?

KATE. Scary. It's going to be close.

JORGENSON. Close? We have forty percent. He has twenty five. We would only need ten of the remaining thirty five. That's less than one in three. If we can't get that — Christ, Richard Nixon could get that.

BEA. *(to KATE:)* Always wanted to be a politician.

JORGENSON. I did. Always wanted to be Harry Truman. God damned son-of-a-bitch just went out and told the truth. *(to BEA:)* And that's what we're going to do. We're going out there and tell the truth. Send a letter to the stockholders? We'll visit them. Hell, we'll even have them over for dinner.

KATE. Harry and Bess hit the campaign trail. *(Begins to leave.)*

JORGENSON. Before you go. You said he gave you two propositions. What was the other?

KATE. Oh, just Garkinkle's idea of a tender offer. Come on. Drive me to the airport. C'mon.

(Blackout. Lights up on GARFINKLE alone in his office. COLES is there, briefcase in hand.)

GARFINKLE. Aw Christ, what do *you* want?

COLES. Good morning, Mr. Garfinkle.

GARFINKLE. Are you about to regale me with the latest saga of Bill Jr., at Columbia?

COLES. Strictly business. As you know I had sixty thousand shares of New England stock when we first met.

GARFINKLE. Excuse me — it'll be a history lesson instead.

COLES. Since becoming aware of your investment I have purchased an additional forty thousand shares. I now have a hundred thousand shares.

GARFINKLE. Congratulations.

COLES. I'm prepared to sell you the right to vote those shares at the Annual Meeting. Are you interested?

GARFINKLE. Sit down. I'm interested. *(COLES sits.)* How much?

COLES. A million.

GARFINKLE. Too much.

COLES. You need a million votes above what you

already own. I can get you ten per cent of the way there in one transaction. Better yet, it's votes they're counting on for themselves. I think what I'm asking is fair.

GARFINKLE. If your shares make a difference — if I win by less than a hundred thousand you got your million. Otherwise I don't need them. I won't vote them.

COLES. I'm not selling you an option. I'm selling you the right to vote the shares. How you vote them, if you vote them, is your business. It's of no concern to me.

GARFINKLE. ... If they make the difference, you got a million. If they don't, half a million.

COLES. Agreed. *(reaching into his briefcase)* I've prepared the papers. I just left the numbers blank. Have your lawyers review it. I'm staying over. I'll pick it up in the morning — along with a check. *(Places papers neatly on GARFINKLE'S desk.)* Good day, Mr. Garfinkle. *(Exits GAR-FINKLE'S office. Moves Center Stage. GARFINKLE shouts after him, a beat after his Exit.)*

GARFINKLE. And how is Bill Jr. doing with his studies? *(Lights out on GARFINKLE. COLES is alone.)*

COLES. Don't look at me like that. Everybody looks out after their own self-interest. "What's in it for me?" Isn't that, ultimately, what it's all about? Jorgenson looks out for his monument. Garfinkle for his money. Bea for her man. Kate for her career. The employees for their paycheck. I kept this company alive. I helped make it all possible. Who looks out for me? *(A burst of MUSIC as lights slowly fade on COLES.)*

(Lights up on BEA as she tries to get her bearings.)

BEA. This way? ... Through there...

(Lights up on GARFINKLE in his office. She Enters.)

BEA. Good afternoon, Mr. Garfinkle.

GARFINKLE. Oh no — the donut thrower. Wait — I got to get my catcher's mask.

BEA. I'm sorry. I didn't bring any.

GARFINKLE. Aw ... And I was looking forward to some of your nutritious health donuts — you know — yogurt sprinkles — penicillin-filled.

BEA. ... These offices are every bit as impressive as my daughter said they were.

GARFINKLE. ... What do you know ... I like your daughter. She's hot shit.

BEA. .. I think so too ... assuming I know what you mean.

GARFINKLE. You know what I mean. She's terrific. And she didn't get that way working for those clowns at Morgan, Stanley. She must've got it from you.

BEA. That's kind of you.

GARFINKLE. Did she send you? I wouldn't put it past her.

BEA. She didn't send me. She would be upset with me if she knew. I expect this meeting will be held in confidence.

GARFINKLE. Have a seat. *(She sits.)* What can I do for you?

BEA. You can take the million dollars I'm about to offer you.

GARFINKLE. *(sitting)* ... This is gonna be some day.

BEA. I thought that might interest you. There is a trust fund, in my name, with a million dollars, primarily in treasury notes, in it. I will turn it over to you if you call off your fight with us. We will buy back your shares at thirteen, which Kate informs me gets you even, plus you'll have a million dollars profit.

GARFINKLE. How come I never had a mother like you?

BEA. Is that acceptable?

GARFINKLE. My mother — I gotta send a check once a month. Would you like to meet her?

BEA. Is that acceptable?

GARFINKLE. How much money you make a year?

BEA. I don't see—

GARFINKLE. How much?

BEA. Forty thousand. Plus health insurance.

GARFINKLE. Why would you give up a million to save forty?

BEA. That's my affair. Is it agreeable to you?

GARFINKLE. Who are you doing it for?

BEA. Myself. I don't need the money.

GARFINKLE. I don't either.

BEA. Then why are you doing it?

GARFINKLE. That's what I do for a living. I make money.

BEA. You will have made money. If you accept my offer you will have made a million dollars. For a few weeks' effort you will have made more than most working a lifetime.

GARFINKLE. Go home. I don't want your money.

BEA. Why? Isn't it good enough for you?

GARFINKLE. It's good. It just not enough.

BEA. I know a million dollars is not a great deal of money to you. It's all I have. If I had more I'd offer you more. I had really hoped to appeal to whatever decent instincts you have left. I'm here to plead for my company.

GARFINKLE. Go home.

BEA. Please, Mr. Garfinkle.

GARFINKLE. I don't take money from widows and orphans. I make them money.

BEA. Before or after you put them out of business?

GARFINKLE. You're getting on my nerves. Go home.

BEA. I intend to. Before I go I'd like to know — I'd like you to tell me — how you can live with yourself?

GARFINKLE. I have no choice. No one else will.

BEA. How? How can you destroy a company ... its people ... for the sake of dollars you don't even need?

GARFINKLE. Because it's there.

BEA. ... Because it's there?

GARFINKLE. What? People climb moutains — swim oceans — walk through fire — 'cause it's there. This way is better. You don't get all sweated up.

BEA. There are people there. There are dreams there—

GARFINKLE. Do you want to give a speech or do you want an answer? 'Cause the answer is not complicated. It's simple. I do it for the money. I don't need the money. I want the money. Shouldn't surprise you. Since when do needs and wants have anything to do with one another? If they did I'd be back in the Bronx and you'd be getting Yorgy his coffee up in Grimetown. You don't need the job. You need the million dollars. But you're prepared to give up what you need — a million dollars — for what you want — a stinking job. You're fucked up, lady. You're sick. Go see a psychiatrist.

BEA. You are the sick one. Don't you know that?

GARFINKLE. Why? 'Cause I know what I want and I know how to get it? Lady, I *looooove* money. I love money more than I love the things it can buy. And I love the things it can buy. You know why? Money is unconditional acceptance. It don't care whether I'm good or not, whether I snore or don't, which God I pray to — it makes me as much interest in the bank as yours does. There's only three things in this world that give that kind of unconditional acceptance — dogs, donuts and money. Only money is better. It don't make you fat and it don't shit all over the living room floor.

BEA. I hope you choke on your money and die! *(She Exits. GARFINKLE smiles sadly.)*

GARFINKLE. How come I always bring out the best in people?

KATE. *(in Conference Room)* You bring out the best in me.

GARFINKLE. I know I do that, Katie, me girl.

KATE. The Irish in me.

GARFINKLE. ... Same thing.

KATE. What's the matter? Are you becoming melancholy on me?

GARFINKLE. Melancholy? Why would you say that? Just 'cause the Governor calls every hour ... the unions are picketing my house ... prayer meetings daily chant for my demise—

KATE. *(moving to his office)* You're in the wrong profes-

sion. You should head the U.N. Nobody can bring people together like you ... not even a chuckle? You must
really be in bad shape. Feeling unloved?

GARFINKLE. Unappreciated. I'm doing the right thing.
I'm taking unproductive assets and making them pro-
ductive. Just following the first law of free enterprise
economics.

KATE. What law is that?

GARFINKLE. Survival of the fittest.

KATE. The Charles Darwin of Wall Street!

GARFINKLE. *(laughing)* ... I like that. The Charles Darwin of Wall Street.

KATE. Maybe they don't see it that way. Maybe they
don't see as survival of the fittest. Maybe they see it as
survival of the fattest.

GARFINKLE. Katie, why are you so hard on me?

KATE. 'Cause you're not nice.

GARFINKLE. Since when do you have to be nice to
be right?

KATE. You're not right. You're "What's happening."
One day we'll smarten up and pass some laws and put
you out of business. Ten years from now they'll be study-
ing you at the Wharton School. They'll call it the "Garfinkle Era" and rinse out their mouths when they leave
the room.

GARFINKLE. That's how you talk about family?

KATE. Family?

GARFINKLE. Immediate family. For every deal I find,
you guys bring me ten. We happen to be in bed together,
lady. Calling it family that's being nice. Look at me,
Kate.

KATE. I'm going to put you away, Garfinkle.

GARFINKLE. I'm not going away. They can pass all the laws they want — All they can do is change the rules — they can't stop the game. I don't go way. I adapt. Look at me, Kate. Look at you. God damn it! We're the same!

KATE. We are not the same. We are not the same! We sit on opposite sides here. I like where I sit. You sit in shit.

GARFINKLE. You sit with me.

KATE. You sit alone.

GARFINKLE. Alone? Get off it, will you? We've come from "Ask not what you country can do for you" to "What's in it for me?" to "What's in it for me — today!" all in one short generation. That's why those stuck-holders all love me and that's why you guys all work for me. Nobody's putting a gun to anyone's head. Everybody's got their hand out.

KATE. Not everybody. Not me. Not them.

GARFINKLE. Forget them. It's about you and me now, Kate. I'm the last thought you have when you fall asleep at night and the first when you wake in the morning. I make your juices flow and you know it.

KATE. Garfinkle, if you knew what you do to me you wouldn't brag about it.

GARFINKLE. And you know what makes the two of us so special? What sets us apart? We care more about the game than we do the players. That's not bad. That's smart.

KATE. That's grotesque. Garfinkle, you don't know me. You're not capable of knowing me. You can't see beyond your appetite.

GARFINKLE. Then what the fuck are you doing here!? You can't keep away. You don't want to keep away. Come ... *play* with me. Be a *play*er — not a technician. Feel the power. This is where you belong. With me. I know you. I know who you are. I like who you are. I want you, Kate.

KATE. *(moving away)* I'm going to nail you, Garfinkle. I'm going to send you back to Wall Street with donuts up your ass and everyone's going to know how some broad wet behind the ears did you. And whatever happens from this day forward, whatever successes I achieve, none — none will be sweeter than this one! *(She Exits. GAR-FINKLE, a beat after the Exit yells to her.)*

GARFINKLE. You're so perfect for me! *(Turns, begins to Exit.)* To be continued. In Grimetown. *(He Exits.)*

(Lights up on JORGENSON alone in his office. BEA Enters, gently singing "Hey, Good Lookin'."* JORGENSON smiles weakly.)

BEA. You OK?

JORGENSON. Just going over in my head what I want to say.

BEA. They're putting speakers out in the hallways. The auditorium won't fit everyone. I feel like we're Harry and Bess on election night.

JORGENSON. Harry was a better man than me. Went to sleep election night. I haven't slept good for days.

BEA. Talk to me.

* Cautionary Note: Permission to produce this play does not include rights to use this song. Producers must secure such permission from its copyright owner.

JORGENSON. I'm scared, Bea. I'm scared time has passed us by. I'm scared I don't know this new environment. I'm scared what I do know doesn't count for anything anymore.

BEA. *(Moves behind him. Rubs his neck.)* I'm not scared. I'm proud. I'm proud of the business we built. Most of all I'm proud of you. And if what we are counts for nothing anymore, that won't be our failing — it'll be theirs. *(He smiles. Squeezes her hand.)* It'll be all right. Just go out and tell the truth. Go out and give them hell, Harry. *(They remain frozen.)*

(GARFINKLE Enters. Looks at them.)

GARFINKLE. The truth? Why don't you tell the truth, lady? The truth is Harry Truman is dead.

(A burst of MUSIC. Lights dim on BEA and JORGENSON though they continue visible. GARFINKLE moves to his darkened office. BEA moves Downstage Center. We're at the Annual Meeting. Scene is played as if audience were the stockholders. KATE, COLES & JORGENSON sit at conference room table.)

BEA. That concludes the formal aspect of our Annual Meeting. The one remaining item of business is the election of directors. Is there anyone entitled to vote who does not have a ballot? Please raise your hand. *(She looks about at the audience.)* Will the inspector of elections distribute the ballots. Please keep your hand raised so you can receive your ballot. Thank you. *(JORGENSON rises from table and moves to Downstage Center.)*

JORGENSON. *(addressing audience as if they were the stockholders)* It's nice to see so many familiar faces ...

old friends ... many of you I haven't seen for years. Thank you for coming and welcome to the 73rd Annual Meeting of New England Wire and Cable — the 38th of which I am addressing you as your Chief Executive.

Bill Coles, our able President, has told you about our year; what we accomplished — where we need to make further improvements — what our business goals are for next year and the years beyond.

I'd like to talk to you about something else. On this, our 73rd year, I'd like to share with you some of my thoughts concerning the vote you are about to make in the company you own.

We've had some very good years. We've had some difficult ones as well. Though the last decade has been troubling for us it's been devastating for our industry. Ten short years ago we were the twelfth largest manufacturer of wire and cable in the country, the fourth largest in New England. We're now the third largest in the country and the largest in New England.

We might not have flourished — but we survived. And we're stronger for it. I'm proud of what we accomplished.

So, we're at that point, where this proud company, which has survived the death of its founder, numerous recessions, a major depression and two world wars is in imminent danger of self-destructing this day in the town of its birth.

And there is the instrument of our destruction. I want you to see him in all his glory. Larry the Liquidator — the entrepreneur in post-industrial America — playing God with other people's money.

(GARFINKLE nods to the audience.)

At least the robber barons of old left something tangible in their wake. A coal mine. A railroad. Banks. This man leaves nothing. He creates nothing. He builds nothing. He runs nothing. In his wake lies nothing but a blizzard of paper to cover the pain.

If he said, "I could run this business better." Well, that's something worth talking about. He's not saying that. He's saying, "I am going to kill you because at this particular moment in time you're worth more dead than alive."

Well maybe that's true. But it is also true that one day this industry will turn. One day when the dollar is weaker or the yen stronger or when we finally begin to rebuild the roads, the bridges, the infrastructure of our country demand will skyrocket. And when those things happen we will be here — and we will be stronger for our ordeal — stronger for having survived. And the price of our stock will make his offer pale by comparison.

God save us if you vote to take his paltry few dollars and

run. God save this country if *(pointing to GARFINKLE)* "that" is truly the wave of the future. We will then have become a nation that makes nothing but hamburgers, creates nothing but lawyers, and sells nothing but tax shelters.

And if we have come to the point in this country where we kill something because at the moment it's worth more dead than alive, then turn around and take a good look at your neighbor. You won't kill him because it's called "murder" and it's illegal. This too is murder, on a mass scale, only on Wall Street they call it "maximizing shareholder values" and they call it legal and they substitute dollar bills where a conscience should be.

Damn it. A business is more than the price of its stock. It is the place where we make our living, meet our friends and dream our dreams. It is, in every sense, the very fabric that binds our society together. So let us, right now, at this meeting, say to every Garfinkle in this land, that here we build things, we don't destroy them. Here, we care for more than the price of our stock. Here ... we care about people. *(JORGENSON moves from lectern back to table. BEA, COLES and KATE stand and applaud. GARFINKLE follows JORGENSON back and as the applause dies, says to BEA, COLES and JORGENSON respectively.)*

GARFINKLE. Amen ... And Amen ... And Amen. Say "Amen," someone, please! *(to audience)* You'll excuse me. I'm not familiar with the local custom ... The way I was brought up you always said "Amen" after you heard a prayer. You hear someone praying, after he finishes, you say "Amen" and drink a little wine.

'Cause that's what you just heard — a prayer. The way I was brought up we called that particular prayer — the prayer for the dead. You just heard the prayer for the dead, and fellow stuckholders, you didn't say "Amen" and you didn't even get to sip the wine.

What — You don't think this company is dead? Steel — you remember steel, don't you? Steel used to be an industry. Now heavy metal is a rock group.

This company is dead. Don't blame me. I didn't kill it. It was dead when I got here. It is too late for prayers, for even if the prayers were answered and a miracle occurred and the yen did this and the dollar did that and the infrastructure did the other thing we would still be dead. Know why? Fibre-optics. New technologies. Obsolescence.

We're dead all right. We're just not broke. And you know the surest way to go broke? Keep getting an increasing share of a shrinking market. Down the tubes. Slow but sure. You know, at one time there must have been dozens of companies making buggy whips. And I'll bet you anything the last one around was the one that made the best god damned buggy whip you ever saw. How would you have liked to have been a stuckholder of that company?

You invested in a business. And that business is dead.

Let's have the intelligence, let's have the decency, to sign the death certificate, collect the insurance and invest the money in something with a future.

Aha — But we can't, goes the prayer — we can't because we have a responsibility — a responsibility to our employees, our community. What will happen to them? I got two words for that — "Who cares?" Care about them? They didn't care about you. They sucked you dry. You have no responsibility to them.

For the last ten years this company has bled your money. Did this Community care? Did they ever say, "I know things are tough. We'll lower your taxes, reduce water and sewer?" Check it out. We're paying twice what we paid ten years ago. And the mayor is making twice what he made ten years ago. And our devoted employees, after taking no increases for three years, are still making twice what they made ten years ago. And our stock is one-sixth what it was ten years ago. Who cares? I'll tell you — me!

I'm not your best friend — I'm your only friend. I care about you in the only way that matters in business. I don't make anything? I'm making you money. And, lest we forget, that's the only reason any of you became stock-holders in the first place. To make money. You don't care if they manufacture wire and cable, fry chicken, or grow tangerines. You want to make money. I'm making you money. I'm the only friend you got.

Take that money. Invest it somewhere else. Maybe — maybe you'll get lucky and it will be used productively — and if it is — you'll create more jobs and provide a service for the economy and God forbid — even make a few bucks for yourself. Let the Governor and the Mayor and the unions worry about what you paid them to worry about. And if anyone asks, tell them you gave at the plant.

And it pleases me that I'm called "Larry the Liquidator." You know why, fellow stuckholders? Because at my funeral you'll leave with a smile on your face ... and a few bucks in your pocket. Now that is a funeral worth having. *(breathing heavily, GARFINKLE pauses a beat and sits)*

BEA. ... Will the inspector of elections please collect the ballots.

(COLES rises, moves slowly Center Stage, addresses audience.)

COLES. That's what happened. That's it. All of it.

BEA. Is there anyone entitled to vote who has not turned in a ballot?

COLES. It's happening everywhere. No one is immune.

BEA. To retain the present Board: 1,741,416.

COLES. I think the old man gave the speech of his life. I can't think how he could have said it better.

BEA. For the opposition slate: 2,219,901.

COLES. What do we do? Pass another law. There's already a law against murder. All he did was supply the weapon.

BEA. Not voting: 176,111.

COLES. Garfinkle won in a landslide. Didn't even need my votes. Cost me the second half million but I feel good about that. I feel better about getting the first half million. I feel best it cost him money he didn't have to spend. That's the only kind of lasting satisfaction you get when you deal with people like him.

BEA. Mr. Garfinkle, your slate is elected.

COLES. He had the nerve to ask me to stay on while he dismembered the company. Even offered me a raise. I said "no" of course. There's a point at which we all draw the line.

JORGENSON. *(in his office)* We can't leave now. I have to tell the men.

BEA. They know.

JORGENSON. ... Already?

BEA. Let's go home. There'll be time tomorrow.

JORGENSON. Even ... Ozzie voted for him. *(He Exits. She remains.)*

COLES. He didn't take it well. From me ... I think he expected it. Ozzie ... Ozzie kind of threw him. With all his money you'd think he would have left. Gone somewhere nice ... somewhere warm. He didn't. Stayed right here. Died almost two years later. Left more than thirty million.

BEA. Jorgy, you only made one mistake in your life. You lived two years too long.

COLES. Bea became executor of his estate. Bought the land the plant used to sit on. Put up a kind of ... Employee Retraining Center — Actually placed a few people ... about a hundred of the twelve hundred or so that worked there when the plant closed. It wasn't easy retraining middle-aged men who are used to working with their hands. Some went to work for McDonald's ... or as night watchmen.

Me? I didn't do too badly. I moved back to Florida. Run a mid-sized division for a nationally know food processor. I won't ever run the company ... but I'm financially secure. And you can't beat the weather.

(Lights up on GARFINKLE. He speaks to KATE who is seated at conference table.)

GARFINKLE. I'm sorry, Kate. I'm surprised myself. See, you do bring out the best in me. Come, ride back to New York with me ... You worried it wouldn't look right? Don't. It's the perfect ending ... Come... Come. *(She doesn't move.)* I got donuts in the car.

COLES. Kate and Garfinkle? Well, three months later, which was as soon as she could work things out at Morgan, Stanley, she went to work for him. *(KATE rises from table and moves to GARFINKLE'S office.)* She was very good. Three months after that she became his partner. *(KATE takes a folder from GARFINKLE and sits at his desk.)* ... then his wife. *(GARFINKLE beams. BEA Exits.)* They have two kids. Set of twins. Call them their "little bull and little bear." Friend of mine saw them the other day ... Said he never saw them happier. *(KATE & GARFINKLE smile at one another. A short burst of MUSIC.)*

BLACKOUT

AUTHOR'S NOTE

The character of Garfinkle can be played many ways. The one way he should not be played is overly, coarsely, "ethnic". Though he boasts of his Bronx upbringing he is an educated man and no doubt has an M.B.A. from some top university. His speech patterns are those of a third-generation New Yorker.

PROP LIST

Wall Street Journal (COLES) Stock pages
Mechanical pencil (COLES) In jacket pocket
Pocket notebook (COLES) In jacket pocket
Briefcase (COLES)
Handkerchief (GARFINKLE)
Roll of cash (GARFINKLE) Real: 1-$10, 1-$5, 3-$1 around
   wad of fakes
Cigarettes (GARFINKLE) Parliament in box
Pocket lighter (GARFINKLE)
White bakery bag (BEA) w/donuts
12 donuts (BEA) Honey/wholewheat
Change ($) (BEA) $1 & 6 coins
Legal pad (COLES) Top of bookcase
Box of pencils (BEA) Brought on
Typing paper (BEA) Brought on
Box of paperclips (BEA) Brought on
Ashtray on conference table
Coffee maker on work table
Tray on work table
4 coffee mugs on tray
Spoon on tray
Sugar in bowl on tray
Small milk bottle, w/milk, on tray
Paper towels on work table
Matches on work table
Whiskbroom & pickeruper next to work table
Trashcan next to work table

Conical paper watercups at watercooler
Trash box next to watercooler
1″ micrometer (JORGENSON) On Jorg. desk
Wire/cable (JORGENSON) Use w/micrometer
File folder (JORGENSON) On Jorg. desk
Pencils in holder
Telephone on Jorg. desk
Wire letter basket on Jorg. desk
Letters in basket
Green shirt (Dressing) over Jorg. chair
Trashcan next to Jorg. desk
Video monitor in Garf. office—Stockquote machine
Keyboard attached to programmed computer
Ashtray on Garf. desk
Tray on Garf. desk
Water pitcher on tray
2 water glasses on tray
Telephone on Garf. desk
Pen on Garf. desk
Pocket lighter on Garf. desk
Parliament cigarettes in box on Garf. desk
3 case files on Garf. desk
Trashcan next to Garf. desk
Eyeglasses (GARFINKLE) On desk
File folder (JORGENSON) Brought on
File folders (JORGENSON) In file cabinet
Gardenia plant (GARFINKLE) Ozzie to Garf.
Baseball cap (Boston) (JORGENSON) On top of book-
    case
Donut machine
Fake donuts on donut machine (raspberry, toasted

coconut, choc. sprinkles, choc. icing, choc. fudge,
choc. cream)
Tray on donut machine
Doiley on tray
3 clumps of fake donuts on tray
Chocolate fudge donut (real) on tray
Briefcase (KATE)
File w/papers (KATE) In briefcase
Pen (KATE) In briefcase
List of things to cover (KATE) In #181 file
Business card (KATE)
2 chocolate fudge donuts in donut drawer
Papers (Tender) (KATE)

ACT 2

Bottle of champagne (Jorg. Office) Filled w/gingerale
4 glasses (Jorg. Office) Water type
Toasted coconut donut (Garf. Office) In donut drawer
2 business reports (Garf. Office) On desk
Yellow pad (BEA)
Pencil (BEA)
File (COLES) In briefcase
Right to vote papers (COLES) In file
3 index cards w/vote results

FURNITURE

Desk, (Jorg. Office)
Desk chair (Jorg. Office) Swivel, casters
Bookcase (Jorg. Office) Divide hall & office

Cabinet (Jorg. Office) Under window
Coat hooks (Jorg. Office) Storage cabinet
Conference table (Jorg. Office)
3 conference chairs (Jorg. Office)
Work table (Jorg. Office)
2 file cabinets (Jorg. Office)
Side chair (Jorg. Office) Under work table
Water cooler (Jorg. Office)
2 side chairs (Jorg. Office) Dressing
Desk (Garf. Office)
Desk chair (Garf. Office) Swivel, casters
Visitor chair (Garf. Office) Swivel, casters
Shelf w/drawer (Garf. Office) for computer & donuts
Meeting chair, L. on grey area, for Garf. in stock-
    market

PERISHABLE LIST

COFFEE in auto drip coffee pot, 3—4 cups per show
SUGAR, 1 cup, replenished every few performances
MILK, 1 cup, replenished every few performances
3 CHOCOLATE DONUTS (Dunkin Donuts—chocolate
  honey dipped)
WATER in water cooler
CONICAL WATER CUPS
Champagne in champagne bottle — GINGER ALE
  enough for four glasses
1 TOASTED COCONUT DONUT (Dunkin Donuts)
CIGARETTES—Parliament in box—approx. 20 per
  performance (10 in each of 2 boxes)
BUTANE for lighter
12 DONUTS— honey/whole wheat in white bakery bag
  (not eaten, can be varnished/dried/stale)
White bakery BAG—1 per show—for donuts
Yellow LEGAL PADS—bound on top
PENCILS
Manilla FILE FOLDERS
File folder LABELS
Legal size ENVELOPES—for J letters
WALL ST. JOURNAL
INDEX CARDS—for vote results
CHAMPAGNE BOTTLE
NOTE PAD—refill for Cole's pocket notebook

DOCUMENT LIST

Manilla FILE FOLDER, slightly worn, containing 10—15 sheets of paper, typewritten

3—4 manilla FILE FOLDERS, worn, containing 10—15 typewritten pages

FILE FOLDER, label on side, relatively new, 10—15 typewritten pages, info on Wire and Cable troubles

BUSINESS CARD

> Kate Sullivan
> Vice President
> Stanley, Morgan

3 CASE FILES, one page on cover with summary of case, to be replaced every show, typewritten pages on the inside

LIST of points to cover
"One: For every share you acquire it's one less Garfinkle can get.
Two: Drive the price of the stock up.
Three: Your liquid balance sheet is attractive as long as you don't go into debt. Debt makes you less attractive.
Four: Get a letter out to the shareholders telling them how great business is. Do not mention a potential takeover.
Five: Anti-takeover legislation— Connections with Governor or other politicians."

LEGAL TENDER, an offer from OPM to buy New England Wire and Cable shares at $20.00 per share. (Booklet with thin pages—blue writing)

RIGHT TO VOTE PAPERS, Consisting of a card and legal contract to sell the right to vote the shares from William Coles to Lawrence Garfinkle, the numbers are left blank to be filled in by Garfinkle.

3x5 INDEX CARDS with vote results, in large dark figures,
"To retain the present Board: 1,741,416
For the Opposition slate: 2,219,901
Not voting: 176,111"

ONSTAGE PRESET

ACT I
GARFINKLE'S OFFICE

DESK
PHONE
ASHTRAY — w/water
TRAY w/
    PITCHER of water—½ full
    2 GLASSES
3 CASE FILES w/COVER SHEETS
    Bottom—Trouble
    Middle—Fuck Them
    Top—They're Morons
PACK of CIGARETTES (10)
Pocket LIGHTER
PEN—closed
EYEGLASSES

COMPUTER TABLE
MONITOR & KEYBOARD—preset to screen #4
2 choc. fudge DONUTS—in drawer
PACK of CIGARETTES (10)—(Backup—in rear of drawer)

DESK CHAIR
Arm parallel to desk—facing SL

VISITOR CHAIR
On farthest SR spike marks—facing slightly SL

TRASH CAN
Underneath desk—DSL side

JORGENSON'S OFFICE

DESK
PHONE
FILE FOLDER—open
MICROMETER & CABLE—on top of folder
PENCIL—on top of folder
PENCIL HOLDER—w/**PENCILS**
Wire **LETTER BASKET**
    LETTERS—in top of basket

DESK CHAIR
Pulled out from desk
GREEN SHIRT—over back of chair

ON HOOKS   ‒
HANGER w/
    J's **SUIT JACKET**—w/**PENCIL** in pocket
J's **TIE**—pretied

DONUT MACHINE
On Offstage Office Platform; handle facing DS &
   Onstage (Masking in place)
TRAY w/3 cluster of **FAKE DONUTS**
REAL choc. fudge **DONUT**—on top of clusters

BOOKCASE
LEGAL PAD—on top, Onstage corner
BASEBALL CAP—on top of wooden box

CABINET
LETTER in wire BASKET—below window—sticking out
    diagionally

TRASH CAN—WIRE
Under US side of J desk

WORK TABLE
COFFEE MAKER w/
    POT of COFFEE—¾ full
TRAY w/
    3 MUGS
    SUGAR BOWL w/sugar
    MILK BOTTLE w/¼ milk
    SPOON
    (POT & ALL MUGS w/handles pointing DSL)
1 MUG—set in front of coffee maker
PAPER TOWELS
MATCHES (backup)
WHISKBROOM & PAN—SL of table

SIDE CHAIR
On spikes (slightly pulled out) under work table

TRASHCAN—GREY PLASTIC
SL of work table

FILE CABINETS (2)
HANGING FILES—W/MANILLA FILES—US Top
  Drawer
Space in front for J to put file

WATERCOOLER
WATER—filled ¾—(once a week or as needed)
CONICAL CUPS—in DISPENSER

TRASH BOX
US of watercooler

CONFERENCE TABLE
ASHTRAY—w/water
3 CHAIRS—SR, SL—pushed in; US—open L side

G BOARD MTG. CHAIR
DSL grey carpet area—on spikes

OFFSTAGE PRESET

ACT I

STAGE RIGHT TABLE

Cole's BRIEFCASE w/
    RIGHT TO VOTE PAPERS in FOLDER

WALL STREET JOURNAL (C)
    Folded to Stock Pages

FILE FOLDER (J)

3 INDEX CARDS w/Vote Results (B)
    Top—To retain the present Board: 1,741,416
    Middle—For the opposition slate: 2,219,901
    Bottom—Not voting: 176, 111

Kate's BRIEFCASE w/
    LIST OF POINTS in FOLDER
    YELLOW PAD SHEET—on top of list of points
    PEN

CHAMPAGNE BOTTLE
    ½ full w/ginger ale

4 WATER GLASSES

PLANT (G)

YELLOW PAD (B)
PENCIL

2 white MUGS (Act 2—Work Table)

2 DOCUMENTS (Act 2—G Desk)

Toasted coconut DONUT (Act 2—G Drawer)

BEHIND SL OFFICE WALL

Legal TENDER (K)
Kate's COAT—on hook (Costumes)

TRAP

BAG of 12 DONUTS (B)

CHANGE—2 $1 & 45¢ (B)

BOX of PENCILS (B)
TYPING PAPER
BOX of PAPER CLIPS

WATER PITCHER w/WATER
CUPS
TISSUES

DRESSING ROOMS

GARFINKLE
HANDKERCHIEF (Costumes)

PACK of CIGARETTES (10)
LIGHTER
CASH
    Bottom—$1
    Middle—fake wad
    Top—$10, $5

COLES
Pocket NOTEBOOK
Mechanical PENCIL

BEA
3 INDEX CARDS — in Suit Pocket *(Backup)*

COSTUME CHANGES

CHARACTER	CHANGE WHERE? (w/help)	TIME
BEA	Pit (no)	6 min.
BEA	Dress Room (no)	11 min.
COLES	Stage Right (1 person)	9 min.
BEA	Dress Room (no)	5 min.
KATE	Stage Left (no)	15 sec.

ACT II

BEA	Dress Room (no)	10 min.
JORG.	Stage Right (no)	10 min.
KATE	Stage Left (2 people)	1½ min.
COLES	Stage Right (no)	2 min.
BEA	Stage Left (1 person)	2 min.
KATE	Dress Room (no)	8 min.
JORG.	Stage Right (no)	8 min.
COLES	Stage Right (1 person)	10 min.
BEA	Dress Room (1 person)	3½ min.

COSTUMES

BEA

ACT I
Pink blouse
Plum paisley skirt
Plum sweater
Burgundy shoes
Pantyhose—Hanes Town Taupe—Sheer
Gold watch
Single pearl earrings
Pearl necklace (throughout)

GOING FOR DONUTS (Pit change)
Add:
    Coat
    Scarf

END OF FIRST GARF. SCENE (Dress Room change)
Cream blouse
Taupe skirt
Brown sweater
Taupe shoes

INTERMISSION (Dress Room change)
Cream blouse
Pink floral skirt
Brown sweater
Taupe shoes

ACT II
END OF CHAMPAGNE SCENE (Dress Room change)
Cream blouse
Plum paisley skirt
Taupe sweater
Burgundy shoes

END OF TO THE AIRPORT (Stage Left change)
Cream blouse
Purple paisley skirt
Taupe pumps
Coat
Scarf
Gloves
Purse

END OF GARF. SCENE (Dress Room change)
Beige suit
Off white blouse w/bow
Taupe pumps

KATE

ACT I
Blue suit w/gold stickpin
White satin blouse
Black pumps
Gold chain, gold earrings
Pantyhose, Hanes Town Taupe

STAGE LEFT CHANGE
Add: Overcoat

INTERMISSION *(Dress Room change)*
Olive suit
Purple silk blouse
Olive shoes
Gold/purple earrings
Gold chain

ACT II
END OF LET'S SETTLE (Stage Left change)
Grey suit w/silver stickpin
Red silk blouse
Silver earrings
Black pumps

END OF AIRPORT (Dress Room change)
Taupe suit
Cream blouse
Silver/cream earrings
Taupe shoes

GARFINKLE

ACT I (No changes)
Grey suit
White shirt
Red suspenders
Red tie
Red hankie
Wrist watch
Ring
Black socks
Black shoes

INTERMISSION (Dress Room change)
Blue suit
Blue & red suspenders
Blue tie
Blue hankie
(White shirt)
(Wrist watch)
(Ring)
(Black socks)
(Black shoes)

ACT II (No changes)

JORGENSON

ACT I
Brown plaid shirt
Brown pants w/beige suspenders
Brown shoes
Lab coat
Grey socks
White T-shirt

ONSTAGE CHANGE
Remove: Lab coat
Add: Sportcoat & striped tie

STAGE RIGHT CHANGE
Remove: Sportcoat & tie
Add: Blue knit cardigan

INTERMISSION (Dress Room change)

Grey plaid shirt
Blue pants w/beige suspenders
Lab coat
Brown shoes

ACT II
END OF TO THE AIRPORT (Stage Right change)
Grey suit
Beige shirt
Blue/red stripe tie
Black shoes

COLES

ACT I
Grey suit
White w/brown & blue stripe shirt
Dk. blue foulard tie
Brown shoes
Navy socks
White T-shirt
Silk pant liners

STAGE RIGHT CHANGE
Blue suit
Stripe shirt (repeat)
Red/gold foulard tie
Black shoes

INTERMISSION (Dress Room change)
Grey suit
White shirt

Blue paisley tie
Brown shoes

ACT II
END OF GOLDEN PARACHUTE (Stage Right change)
Add: Trenchcoat

END OF GARF. SCENE (Stage Right change)
Blue suit
White shirt (repeat)
Navy tie
Black shoes